More Than My Thoughts

Breaking Free From The Grip Of Negative
Thinking and False Beliefs

Scott W Possley

Imperfection Wellness

Copyright

An Imperfection Wellness Edition
ImperfectionWellness.com

Copyright © 2025 by Scott W. Possley

All rights reserved. No part of this book may be reproduced, distributed, transmitted, or stored in a retrieval system in any form or by any means, whole or part, or by any means, including photocopying, recording, or other electronic or mechanical methods, without the prior written permission of the publisher, except by a reviewer, who may quote brief passages in a review and in certain other noncommercial uses, as permitted by copyright law. For permission requests, write to Info@ImperfectionWellness.com with the subject line, "Attention: Copyright Permission."

Ordering Information: Quantity sales. Special discounts are available on quantity purchases by educators, healthcare organizations, and others. For details, please email the publisher at the address above. Orders by U.S. trade bookstores and wholesalers, please email the publisher at the address above.

The author of this book is not dispensing medical advice or prescribing the use of any technique as a form of treatment for physical, emotional, or medical problems without the advice of a physician or other trained medical or mental health provider, either directly or indirectly. The material in this book is intended for educational purposes only and the intent of the author is only to offer information of a general nature for your overall well-being. It is not meant to take the place of diagnosis and treatment by a qualified medical practitioner or therapist. No expressed or implied guarantee of the effects of the use of the recommendations can be given or liability taken. In the event you use any of the information in this book for yourself, the author and the publisher assume no responsibility for your actions.

Library of Congress Cataloging-in-Publication Data
Possley, Scott William.
More Than My Thoughts / by Scott William Possley.
Hardcover ISBN: 979-8-9911786-1-7
Paperback ISBN: 979-8-9911786-0-0
eBook ISBN: 979-8-9911786-2-4

Library of Congress Control Number: 2024925885
First Printing, March 2025

Cover design by Scott William Possley

Acknowledgments

Mom, Dad, Mary & Sherry, thank you for always being so supportive of me. Words can't express my love and gratitude for you each and every day.

The gift of sharing and spreading knowledge in the world is the most noble, so to the many **teachers** in my life, formally and informally, I say thank you!

Allie, you received the first draft and have been there every step of the way since. For that, and so much more, I am beyond grateful—thank you!

To **Andrea, Bob, Missy, Steph** and **Tyler**, thank you for all the feedback and insights of the many drafts and edits that have led to the culmination of this book.

Teri, I'll never forget that fateful night that we talked. Thank you for talking me off the ledge that night which brought me back to living!

Dr. Herbert Robbins, my former therapist, who used to say to me, "Friends are people who know you and like you anyway." I always loved that. It goes along with all of us being *PERFECTLY* Imperfect. Dr. Robbins was there for me at a time when I couldn't see a way out, and he is one of many who helped me on my journey, pulling me out of one of the darkest moments in my adult life. Thank you, Herbert!

And to my friends who have known me and liked me anyway, I am eternally grateful for your unconditional love and support—thank you!

Dedication

This book is dedicated to all of us who have ever felt lost or less than, who have thought they were broken, have suffered or are suffering in silence or have contemplated or tragically have ended their lives by suicide.

We are not alone and we are not broken. Whether you have had a bad day or are using drugs and alcohol to numb in order to get through another day, there is a path and a plan to help you get unstuck from your thoughts, improving your mental health and well-being, and getting you back to living your life to the fullest with contentment and fulfillment from within.

This book is for all of us!

One of the greatest atrocities to affect humankind is that we believe what our thoughts say about us and the world around us.

Scott W Possley

Contents

Preface

There's a voice within all of us. It's a constant narrator shaping how we see ourselves and the world around us. Sometimes, it's kind and encouraging, reminding us of our strength and resilience. Other times, it's harsh and critical, casting doubt on our worth or abilities. And other times, it is boastful and arrogant, telling us we're better than "them." We often mistake this voice for the truth, forgetting it is simply a collection of thoughts. These thoughts, driven by our ego, the part of us that helps us identify self versus other, create the stories we tell ourselves about who we are and what we can or cannot achieve. Often times, this voice gives us our worth and it can just as easily take it away.

From a young age, we begin crafting these narratives, absorbing messages from the people and environments around us. Some of these stories serve us well, motivating us to grow and thrive. But many of them do not. They become self-limiting beliefs; persistent scripts running quietly in the background of our minds, shaping our self-worth, relationships, and understanding of the world.

And there's good news here. These stories are not permanent. They are not who we are, they are mere aspects of us that we can begin to observe. This book, More Than My Thoughts, is for everyone, because we all have thoughts shaped by ego. This book is an invitation to step into awareness, to realize that we are not our thoughts but something far greater. Whether your inner voice whispers words of self-doubt or shouts messages of superiority, the journey toward freedom begins in the same place: recognizing the voice, understanding it, and learning to live beyond it; separate from it.

Possley's Paradigm is introduced in this book, and it offers a roadmap to help you move from "I am my thoughts" to "I have thoughts that pass, and I know am separate from them." It's a guide to breaking free from the grip of egoic thinking and embracing a life of authenticity, contentment and fulfillment from within.

The Stories We Tell Ourselves

We all carry stories within us. Some are so deeply ingrained that we mistake them for reality. The stories we tell ourselves shape how we see ourselves, others, and the world around us. These beliefs whisper, "I'm better than you," "I'm not enough," "I can't do this," or "I don't deserve love." Often, these beliefs are born from early experiences. Perhaps you internalized the idea that your worth depended on how well you performed in school, sports, or other areas of life. Maybe a parent or caregiver, without meaning to, withheld love or approval when you didn't meet certain expectations. Over time, these moments became the foundation of a belief system; a framework of thoughts that now guides your actions, often without you even realizing it.

And then there's the comparison trap, reinforced by the world around us. Social media offers curated glimpses into others' lives, leaving us feeling as though we'll never measure up. The voice in our head reminds us of every shortcoming, magnifying their significance while minimizing our strengths. These limiting beliefs are only one side of the coin.

The Other Side of Ego

While some thoughts tell us we're "less than," other thoughts overcompensate, creating inflated stories about our worth. These thoughts are also ego-driven, designed to shield us from vulnerability or self-doubt.

Perhaps you've heard that inner voice whisper, "I'm smarter, more capable, or better than they are." It might show up in the workplace, where you dismiss a colleague's ideas to strengthen your own competence, which you are insecure about. Or it could emerge as a personal attack, where the ego fosters an us vs. them mentality, convincing you to think, "Since they're different from me, I'll make them the problem. I'll falsely elevate myself by pointing out their flaws, creating division where there could be understanding and connection."

This divisive mindset, born from fear, keeps us separated, reinforcing the illusion that we are fundamentally different from one another. But the truth is, there is far more that unites us than divides us. Beneath the stories of the ego, we are all part of an "us"; connected by our shared humanity and the universal experience of having thoughts and feelings. The ego clings to division, afraid to let go of the identities and judgments that keep us apart. Yet, when we move beyond fear, we can come together, appreciating our differences as strengths rather than reasons for separation. In this way, we transcend divisiveness and create space for understanding, compassion, and unity.

This tendency to inflate our worth doesn't come from a place of malice. We are influenced by the news and media and other fear-driven narratives that fuel division instead of unity. It's a protective mechanism, based in ego, that we are not even aware of; a way to shield ourselves from the fear that maybe we're not enough. By placing ourselves above others, we create a false sense of security. But this security is fleeting, ultimately disconnecting us from genuine relationships and preventing personal growth.

The ego's influence doesn't stop there. It sneaks into how we view success, relationships, and even our struggles. Perhaps you've found yourself comparing achievements, thinking, "I've worked harder for what I have than they ever did." Or maybe you've judged someone else's mistakes, reassuring yourself, "I'd never make that choice. How could they live like that?" These narratives, though subtle, create walls. They isolate us, keeping us from connection and humility. The paradox of the ego is this: Whether it tells us we're "less than" or "better than," it keeps us disconnected from our true selves.

A Roadmap to Authenticity

Possley's Paradigm offers a roadmap for this journey. It's not a quick fix or a one-size-fits-all solution. Instead, it's a set of principles designed to help you separate from the ego and reconnect with your authentic self. By applying the paradigm's concepts, you'll learn to observe your thoughts without judgment, questioning their validity and releasing the grip they have on your life. You'll discover the freedom that comes from living as the observer of your mind rather than its prisoner and begin connecting with people in more authentic ways, beyond the grip of the ego's fear-based thinking. This journey isn't about achieving perfection, it's about embracing the fullness of who you are. It's about embracing your imperfections, uncertainties and all. It's about shifting from "I need more" or "I am better than them" to "I have enough, I am enough, just as I am and there's room at the table for all of us despite our differences."

An Invitation

As you read this book, I invite you to approach it with curiosity and kindness. There's no judgment here, only the recognition that we are all human, navigating the complexities of our minds and hearts. This is not a self-help book in the traditional sense. It's a call to remember a universal truth that has always been within you: You are whole. You are worthy. And you are so much more than your thoughts. Let this book be a companion on your journey, a guide to uncovering the life that's already waiting for you, free from the constraints of egoic thinking. Fulfillment isn't something you achieve; it's something you uncover by living authentically, aligned with your true self. You don't have to be anyone else or anywhere else to begin this journey. You are enough, right here, right now.

Introduction

I moved to New York City in 1999 to study to be a Physician Assistant. Initially, I had a plan of returning to the Midwest after my studies, but after a couple of years, I was hooked on living in New York City. As a gay man growing up in a conservative rural farming town, living there was liberating and freeing. I felt I could achieve anything. I climbed the corporate ladder in healthcare, ultimately moving to the administrative side and working in upper management. On paper, I was the epitome of success. I had the corporate career with a title, a nice salary and great benefits. I lived in a beautiful apartment in Chelsea, and had "made it" in NYC.

While I was grateful for this success, there was a dark secret no one knew. I had little to no self-worth, and I felt nothing on the inside. I felt isolated and alone. When I was with a group of people, I felt like I was on the outside looking in. My thoughts told me this, and I believed it for so many years. All the success I had on the outside for people to see meant nothing to me. I felt numb and dead inside, and I wanted it all to end. I wanted it to go away. I felt broken, and I didn't want to feel broken anymore, but nothing that I did worked. As much as I tried, the thoughts only became louder and meaner, and I continued living in a cycle of feeling worthless and alone with fleeting moments of joy.

My depression, fear and anxiety hid in plain sight, and I became the ultimate chameleon. I was always trying to be who I thought people wanted me to be, and many times, I was failing miserably. Yes, I had plenty of wonderful and sincerely beautiful times with people, but those times were clouded and masked by pain, self-loathing, and feelings of worthlessness that started when I was a child.

Knowing how much I had, and not feeling it on the inside, only made me feel even worse. "How can the guy who has everything feel like he has nothing? What's wrong with me? How ungrateful am I being? Why do I feel so isolated, so broken?" Over time I came to realize why. It was because I was associated with and was attached to my ego and my egoic thoughts and self-beliefs that said I was less than. I was identified as one with that "voice" in my head. The voice of the thoughts that would say, "You are not enough. Nobody will like you if they know the real you." I falsely believed that if the thoughts were coming from me, then they were me. I had a direct association with them and was identified as one with them.

It took me years of struggling to finally learn that I was more than what my thoughts say about me and the world around me. I learned that I am separate from my thoughts. While I have thoughts and self-beliefs, and they are coming from me, or rather my egoic self, I am separate from them. I learned that I can become the observer of them, and separate from the direct association with my thoughts. These realizations were a game changer for me. Over time, I learned to live with my ego and observe its random stream of thoughts filled with comparisons, stories and half-truths, instead of being associated as one with those thoughts and what my ego said about me and the world around me. I was elated to have such a revelation. It turned out that I wasn't broken, and I wasn't crazy. I was human just like everyone else. I felt lighter and happier and returned to living and embracing life.

As great as this felt, there were many times after this revelation when I would fall back into association with my egoic thoughts. This was frustrating for me, and I would feel defeated and deflated. One day I had a revelation that I needed to create a one-page roadmap or cheat sheet that I could easily reference to help me in these moments of despair. One day I drafted a list of concepts, which helped me not only identify when I was associated as one with these thoughts, but the concepts helped me actively disengage from these intrusive thoughts when they arose. This was the genesis of Possley's Paradigm, and later, the creation of ImperfectionWellness.com, Wellness for the *PERFECTLY* Imperfect.

Possley's Paradigm is comprised of ten universal truths that I have put into nine pillars. When applied, in any order, they will help you get unstuck from pervasive, ruminating negative thoughts and self-beliefs, creating a more calm, confident and fulfilled version of you that feels authentic contentment and fulfillment from within. I do not claim any ownership of the individual concepts in the paradigm. I have presented them here as my interpretations of these concepts, which have helped me get unstuck from my negative, ruminating thought patterns, bringing me back to present moment living.

Section I of the book is my background. It goes into some greater detail about my personal life, and how I attached to my thoughts and let them carry me on a wild ride of numbing intoxication, fear, anxiety and depression. I share these details here because I don't want others to feel like they are alone, broken or unfixable. The paradigm has helped me immensely in my life and that is also my wish for you. All humans, with few exceptions, go through association with their thoughts (and for the remainder of the book, if I say thoughts, it means thoughts, feelings, emotions and self-beliefs; anything that makes you believe you are less than in some way), and that is why this book is for everyone.

Section II of the book is Possley's Paradigm. These are the universal truths and core concepts that helped me get unstuck from my thoughts. The paradigm serves as a reference tool and a roadmap for coming back to present moment living. I always keep the paradigm handy. I still use the concepts daily in some form. I have been using it for so long that while I have it memorized and can talk about it for hours on end, there are times when those insidious thoughts from the sly ego, always waiting on the sidelines, pounce when I least expect it, sending me into a tailspin. I grab my copy of the paradigm or walk through it in my head, and within minutes I feel relief. Instead of having a bad day or several bad days, the moment now passes much more quickly, with much less intensity.

It is through a simple shift in how we associate with our thinking that we can become happier and more fulfilled in our daily living. I still have bad days, as that's life and a part of life, but I now have a new found hope. I now have an inner-fulfillment and a stronger foundation that I have never felt before in my life. One day I was overwhelmed with sadness and suddenly I began smiling. I have never had two polar opposite emotions at the same time before. I always thought they were mutually exclusive from each other. I realized it was the paradigm in action. While I was having a bad day, I now knew that it would pass and I was more than this experience and what my thoughts were saying about me. That is when a smile appeared. It is possible to have the two emotions. They do not have to compete with each other; they can co-exist with each other.

I also want to share that I am not a mental health provider. I am trained as a physician assistant and have studied wellness on my own. I have struggled with mental health issues and major depression. Through my struggles, I saw aspects of this paradigm in books, webinars, from therapists and from my meditation training. I put this paradigm together to help others because I do not feel there is anything out there that brings all of these truths into one place as an easy reference. Think of the paradigm as an individualized action plan for YOU...for US! The ideas represented here are age-old and not created by me. I put them into a framework that worked for me and I share them freely with you. I believe mental health is a human right, and as such, we need to have free resources to help anyone who needs them.

Lastly, as part of owning my own imperfection, I want to acknowledge that I am writing, editing and self-publishing this book. I say this because I know after publishing it, I will find a typo, grammatical error or punctuation error. That will be my imperfection out in the open for all of you to see. Instead of NOT moving forward and publishing this, waiting for it to be "perfect," a term only my ego believes in nowadays, I am going to hit submit. And I hope the message, which is intentionally repetitive throughout the book, and my passion for sharing these universal truths, comes through louder than a spelling error or typo, as I want to help others who have struggled in silence like I have for so much of my life.

I hope you enjoy this book and can begin the journey of separating from your thoughts. I hope you can find more contentment and fulfillment in your daily life. If you are someone who has felt broken in the past, or have felt like you are stuck, or felt like you were always on the outside looking in, know you are not alone and there is a way out. Today is a new day and it begins now!

With gratitude,
Scott

Learn more at ImperfectionWellness.com.

Part I: The Road to an Awakening

1

Identification with my Thoughts

W riting a book on wellness was something I never thought I would do. How could someone like me, someone who felt broken and lost, climb out of the depths of despair, finding hope and a love of life I never knew I had in me? Thankfully I was able to! I am about to share a journey of struggles, hope, strength and despair with you, along with a plan for getting unstuck from what our pervasive thoughts say about us and the world around us.

Looking back at my life, the depression, anxiety and fear I had for so many years came from being so engrossed, entangled and aligned as one with my thoughts and self-beliefs, and the horrible things they said about me. I believed those thoughts, and I was caught in a four-decade cycle of ups and downs. I often felt like I was broken and unfixable, but in the end, it turned out I wasn't.

It all came to a head one day early on during the Covid Pandemic in August of 2020. I was at a beach house with friends in Fire Island, New York. I was having an amazing time, yet I felt a strange wave of calm come over me. Out of nowhere, an overwhelming sadness swept over me, and in this calm, I knew the time had finally come to make it all go away. And it felt so incredibly wonderful. I finally had a plan to end my life that night and end my 40 years of suffering.

I was born in a small farming town in rural Illinois two hours southwest of Chicago. Our town was literally surrounded by corn fields. I grew up in a household with two older sisters and two parents who loved each other and all of their children. My cousins on both sides of the family lived across town and we all would gather on numerous family occasions. My maternal and paternal grandparents also lived in town with us. Family and close family bonds were a part of my life growing up. While I didn't know what true unconditional love was until the age of 20 when I came out as gay, I knew growing up that I was in a loving household. Throughout the years, I realized it was this unconditional love that kept me going when I didn't think I could do so myself.

Being born gay and knowing from a very young age was a challenge. It was so hard growing up in a rural conservative farming town with a strict Catholic upbringing. I always felt like I was different, like I was born wrong and that I was broken. I felt like an outsider looking in, and that there was something inherently wrong with me. At the time, that was the message I was sent by the world around me, and I believed it. My immediate family and many of my friends were never overtly mean to me directly, but casual comments from the world at large at the time on "gays and faggots" hurt and created big fears in my mind which I believed for many years.

One day, a close family friend said, "If I ever found out my brother was gay, I'd disown him." I sat there dumbfounded, fearful and sad that someday I would be such a topic of conversation. I saw on the news the many popular anti-gay slogans of the time; the one burnt in my memory was, "AIDS kills fags dead." It was the early 80's and the AIDS epidemic was in the news and in casual discussions constantly. It was ever-present in my small world. The innocence and joy I had felt in the earlier years of my life were slowly being taken away as I started to hide and be ashamed of who I was. I had a secret and believed that no one would ever know. It was then that I began hating who I was. The negative thoughts about myself started at this time, and sadly I believed what these thoughts said about me.

Being gay was something some people suspected, but it was also something I could hide and many never knew. As it was something I could hide, a deep-seated cloud of shame was cast upon me. For years, I tried to "pray the gay away", only to be left tortured that I was stuck with this. I was far from accepting this about myself. My thoughts told me I wasn't good enough, smart enough, good looking enough, and that I was born wrong. My self-worth was nothing and I felt like I was born broken.

Negative thoughts can be pervasive for many people, regardless of how we identify. We each have our story of why we associate with our thoughts. *In the end, it doesn't matter, because these thoughts are not true for any of us.* At the time, though, I didn't know everyone at some point has been tortured by associating with their thoughts. I thought I was the only one. The thoughts said things like, "People are talking about you behind your back. You are a joke. You are too much for people. You are worthless!" The list of insults would go on and on. Sadly, I believed these ever-present negative thoughts as if they were a part of who I was. Why wouldn't I believe the thoughts? They were coming from me!

Throughout my childhood, my mother was an ever-loving protector of her children. I was the youngest of three and the only boy. I didn't stray far from her in unfamiliar situations. This was part of why school was so hard for me. In later years, my mom would recall stories of the many stomachaches I had when starting kindergarten. She finally caught on that I was faking it, until one day it no longer worked. It was then that I began dreading school. Dreading each morning and waiting for the day to end. The dread of going to school would sadly last for many years until I went to college. I just never felt safe and it was a daily hell of going through the motions that felt so insincere.

By second grade, the bullying started with schoolmates calling me "faggot" in the hallways and while walking down the street. Whether or not they knew, the word stung because maybe they were onto me. When I was around 14 years old, I was ambushed by a group of guys from my class who knocked me down and beat me up. I ran home crying and went into my room and shut the door to hide. What was I going to say to my parents? That I was beaten up for being gay? No! I was so afraid my parents would disown me and hate me, thinking it was a choice, when I knew it was just how I was born. I had to hide in silence, and the shame I felt only grew stronger over the years.

At a Catholic grade school, I learned prayers and novenas and said the rosary so many times that it was second nature. I would pray every night begging God to make me "normal." It was futile, and just left me feeling defeated and deflated as a person. Since the prayers never worked, the plan was to live in silence and eventually end my life to end this daily suffering. All the while, that negative voice of those thoughts within would grow and my attachment to them would continue on for many years.

Around third grade, I have memories of a deep sadness settling in. I didn't call it depression, but I knew I was anxious, stressed and sad. I started acting out and didn't know why. I would get in trouble and be asked, "Why did you do that?" To which I replied, "I don't know." And I didn't. I really didn't know why, but it was some sort of release because it felt good on some level whether I realized it or not.

I was still in grade school the first time I contemplated suicide. I remember that day vividly. It was the winter of 1985, and I was in sixth grade. We were in Mrs. Elston's classroom and the radiator heat was too hot so she asked me to open a window, high on the second floor of the school. When I opened the window, the screen fell out and I watched it fall to the ground. A peace came over me realizing I could jump out the window and just end it all. I could end the shame, the embarrassment and the self-hatred that I had for being born this way. It was a perfect solution because no one would ever know that I was gay and I just wanted the pain to end. I thought, if I jump, maybe they will think it was an accident and they will never know my secret. I was staring down on the snowy ground a couple of floors down for what seemed like forever, but it must have been seconds. Mrs. Elston said, "Scott, please sit back down," at which point I walked away from the window feeling deeply that I had missed my moment.

From then on, I learned how to pass through life and survive the day relatively unscathed. It was a series of ups and downs, longing for the school days to end and for the summer to be here. This lasted all throughout grade school and was made even worse when I had to go to high school. I was so relieved when I was able to finally make it to college and escape from this daily hell I was living. While the problems followed me, they were kept at bay for some time. I was able to focus on school and was now making choices for my future, and when I was at college, life felt limitless for the first time in a very long time. I had confidence that I could do what I set my mind to, and I set my sights on graduating and having a career. I thought if I achieved that goal, everything else would fall into place. For the most part it did, as the negative thoughts would sometime be hiding on the sidelines, but they would always return as would my association with them. This continued to follow me throughout college and many years after.

A New Beginning

I got into a physician assistant program in New York and moved to Long Island in 1999. In 2000, I moved to New York City, loving everything it had to offer, but found many social situations to be overwhelming. I quickly realized a few drinks neutralized my thoughts and my attachment to them. Thankfully, my social anxiety temporarily disappeared after I got a little buzz going. I could have a few drinks, and suddenly I would feel okay in my skin. While the drinking was casual in the beginning, over time, it became my crutch. Though the negative thoughts always returned, the alcohol helped keep them at bay long enough for me to enjoy many good times that New York City had to offer.

In 2007, I temporarily left New York City. I went to undergrad in St. Louis, MO, and had friends there from my college years. I was convinced that if I moved back to St. Louis, my problems would be solved, thinking I just need to move and everything will be better. I quickly learned that moving doesn't solve any problems or end those pervasive, ruminating thoughts. They may hide out for a while, but they follow you wherever you go. The move only made things worse, and again, I tried to hide my depression from everyone.

For a year and a half, I lived in St. Louis and the negative voice of my thoughts grew exponentially in that short time. One night was especially bad. I regretted moving and was so overwhelmed that I just started drinking by myself, hoping the pain would go away. That night I was drinking to get drunk, but it didn't numb me in the way I wanted it to. I remember getting into a car to drive a couple of blocks to a gas station to buy a pack of cigarettes. Interestingly enough, I didn't even smoke. And that night I broke my cardinal rule. I was drunk and lost in a state of confusion and I drove anyway because I thought the cigarettes would help me feel something. I drove so slowly and prayed that I wouldn't hurt anyone on the road or get into an accident. I just needed the cigarettes, and the belief in my thoughts convinced me that what I was doing was fine. I chose to do what I did and I accept responsibility for my poor choice, but when under the spell of the manipulative inner-voice, I didn't realize just how poor my choices and how risky my actions were.

Thankfully, I got back to my house safely, and I stood outside smoking as it started to rain. Standing out in the rain getting soaked felt cathartic and cleansing. I started crying and just sat in the rain, lost, depressed, numb and sad. But it was during this moment that I had the clarity that St. Louis did not solve, but only worsened my problems.

After that night out in the rain, a random act of kindness changed my life. My college friend, Grace, happened to move across the street from me, and I gave her a cleaner, abridged version of the story from a couple of nights prior. She was so supportive as she listened and empathized with me. She told me about a book I had to read called, The Power of Now by Eckhart Tolle. After reading the book, I read his second book, A New Earth. I devoured that book, underlining and folding pages, re-reading passages to try and understand human nature from his perspective.

I was also reading books by Lama Surya Das, Wayne W. Dwyer, Thich Nhat Hanh, Pema Chodron and David Hawkins to name a few. These books were life changing, because they shared many of the universal truths that became Possley's Paradigm. It was during this time that I started learning about my thoughts; that inner saboteur voice in my head. For the first time I realized that I wasn't broken after all. I realized that everyone has these thoughts. Some people just get "stuck" or "glued" to them more than others. This is also when I started learning more about the ego and these egoic thoughts. I found out that these thoughts are a part of human nature and are fragments and stories from the past and future that we tell ourselves. While this awareness was wonderful, it would be years before I was able to fully separate from feeling identified as one with my thoughts.

Eventually I left St. Louis and returned to New York City in December 2009, just in time for New Year's Eve 2010. It was great being back home. I re-connected with friends and was back working in healthcare. I had a renewed sense of self and was growing, still with the setbacks and personal struggles of identification with my thoughts, but it wasn't as bad as it was before. I even met a guy and started dating.

Sadly, within weeks, the honeymoon of happiness wore off and I was back to living in my mind identified as one with my thoughts and feelings. As great as this guy was and as much as I wanted to be with someone, I pushed him away. I met more great guys over the years, and continued to push each one away, one by one. The egoic thoughts had control. As much as I wanted to date, the thoughts had other plans. I was so lost in thought that I pushed many a beautiful person away from me, when that was all I had wanted; a beautiful relationship. One-night stands and drinking became the norm again, and each time I thought I found "the one," self-sabotage would leave me alone and empty, turning to food and alcohol to heal the wounds.

While I was still struggling personally, professionally it looked like I had it all. I was promoted to a new role and left my old job, going to work at a new hospital. I even bought a beautiful one-bedroom apartment on the Upper West Side of Manhattan with private outdoor space a block from Central Park. I couldn't believe it. I thought I had finally made it and was "fixed," but the voice sat silently on the sidelines watching and waiting to return. It wouldn't have to wait long.

Over time, the new job was a challenge, and after several months at the new apartment, the challenges at work and owning an apartment in a NYC coop run by incompetent people left me overwhelmed and lost yet again. It was during this time that I really associated with what I call my victim-martyr cycle. "Why do bad things always happen to me? I can't catch a break. Why couldn't things just go easily for me?" The truth was, I had so many breaks, and I was very successful. So many good things did happen for me and many things did go easily for me. I now know in hindsight the immense privilege I had, but at the time, I didn't feel it.

My ego convinced me I had been wronged, that I was the victim. This was the most maddening part of it all. This time the thoughts came, saying, "How could I have so much and still feel nothing on the inside? Where did the happy feelings go? Am I broken? Will I always be lost and searching? What's wrong with me? I have everything and I'm just being a spoiled brat about all this! Get over it already!" And while no one ever said this to me, this is what I thought people thought about me, and what I thought about myself.

Over the years, I bounced back and forth, in and out of depression, trying to make it through the day. The times in my life I was actively suicidal, the only reason I didn't go through with it was because I knew it would devastate my mother. I knew it would devastate many people, but momma Nancy was like no one else in my life. Her unconditional love was the only thing that prevented me from doing the unthinkable.

People say things like, "Suicide is a cop-out. You're going straight to hell. How could you be so selfish? It's a permanent solution to a temporary problem!" What they fail to understand is that when someone is on the brink and con-templating suicide, at least in my case, I felt like I was living a daily hell and was 100% associated with my thoughts. I thought I was what my thoughts told me. I didn't want to die; I just wanted the hidden internal mental pain and anguish to stop. But the thoughts never stopped! They just kept coming, like they do for everyone. The problem was, I believed what my negative thoughts said. I believed I was worthless and shouldn't be here anymore. I was living in a false, painful reality, posing as one thing, feeling like another, and I no longer had any hope for a better tomorrow. Hope had been taken away because of my beliefs that I was one with my thoughts, feelings and emotions. I believed at the time that the horror of each day would be repeated endlessly. It kept me in a locked and fearful state that was at times debilitating. And no one else had any idea!

In the many moments of happiness that I did feel over the years, the hardest part was at the end of the night. The party, dinner or event would end, and I then went home to an empty apartment. The feelings of joy I had when out with friends or family soon ended when I was alone. Unanswered phone calls and texts to friends felt like a thousand daggers, making me second guess if so & so really liked me, or if I was just a bother as my thoughts would tell me. An emptiness would envelope me and that was when the thoughts would go on an all-out attack. It was ruthless, and I just couldn't do it anymore! I was done feeling stuck and without hope. I had fought for so many years and I was tired of feeling this way. I just wanted these thoughts and feelings to go away once and for all.

In August 2020, I was staying with friends in the Fire Island Pines for the week. Fire Island is a beautiful place, and in the summer, it's an oasis on the water. Being at the beach with my friends was extra special that year. It was the first-time groups were allowed to gather after the initial shut-down due to the pandemic. We didn't know much about the pandemic, other than we kept thinking the end was in sight. Living alone and being so isolated, I was relieved that "the worst was behind us" (so we thought) and we would be able to use our summer beach rental for the week. I remember that trip very well, or at least the details of that fateful night.

One night we were in the living room, singing and dancing and drinking, being carefree as ever. It was an amazing time and I was surrounded by amazing people. Suddenly, out of nowhere, I felt cut off from the group. I knew the time with them would be fleeting, ending in several days, and I would have to return to the isolation of my apartment for an unknown time frame that seemed unbearable. This pulled me out of the present moment experience so quickly that I didn't even know what had happened.

The feelings of sadness and loneliness swept over me like a heavy dark cloud. I sat down on the couch and was emotionally out of the room already, though I pretended everything was fine, forcing engagement and laughter. Instantly, I felt so isolated and separate from everyone, despite being five feet from all of them. It was then that I suddenly felt a blanket of warmth and calm come over me. It was so comforting and peaceful and one of the most serene feelings that

I have ever felt. I felt like I was literally being called home to the ocean. I felt so warm and light and happy and liberated that it would finally all be over.

The ocean was less than a five-minute walk away, and all I had to do was get a bit more drunk, weigh myself down with some rocks, and walk into the ocean and finally end it all—end all the pain, end all the suffering, end the never-ending thoughts that said I wasn't enough. It made total sense to me at the time, and logistically I knew I could do it. It just felt so right. Even my ego was satisfied this time. The warmth and comfort that came over me in that moment was the most amazing feeling I'd ever had. It felt so wonderful and serene. In fact, it felt so right that immediately I knew it was wrong. I knew this wasn't the answer, despite how great this idea made me feel. I grabbed my phone, stepped out onto the front porch, and called one of my lifelines.

I knew I had to call Teri, a best friend from grade school. We had shared our struggles in life with each other over the years. It was always without judgment; just pure support for each other and it still is to this day. Teri answered the phone in her usual sassy sarcastic way and she knew something was wrong. She asked, "Are you ok?" And I responded, "No!" And just like that, we started talking as we would have with any other conversation. We just talked to each other without any judgment. I told her what was happening and how I was feeling, and she was just there. She was present in such an amazing way. She wasn't negating or trying to fix anything. She was on the phone with me, creating a safe space to talk in an open and honest way. We reminisced about old times and laughed and cried. It was beautiful, and exactly what I needed.

An hour or so passed, and so did the idea of wanting to end my life. The feelings of inadequacy and lack of self-worth were still there, but I no longer wanted to end my life. There was no longer a desire to end my life that night. I was no longer being called home to the ocean. I promised her I would call her if this ever happened again, and that I would never kill myself.

Eventually, someone from the house popped their head outside to check on me because I had been gone quite a while, and I threw on my chameleon smile and said, "Oh yes, everything is fine, I'll be right in, just finishing a call." Teri laughed and said, "If they only knew," and we both started laughing. I thanked Teri, told her how much I loved and appreciated her, and I ended the call. I walked back into the party, no one the wiser of what had just transpired, and I have not been actively suicidal since.

The next few years were filled with more moments of clarity as well as the usual struggles. From that low point that night, I would take a couple steps forward, backpedal a few steps, but the momentum continued to carry me forward. I had learned Vedic meditation back in 2015, and it resonated so nicely with me that in 2022, I decided to become a meditation teacher. It was during the kick-off weekend of training in January 2023 that so much would change for me.

We finished the first day of meditation teacher training and then came back on Sunday for a half day. At the end of this, we had a group meditation, my first one in over eight years. I knew there was power in group meditation, but I had no idea of what was about to happen. I closed my eyes and started meditating with the group. Instantly, an emotional surge came over me. Tears flowed like they never have before and for 20 minutes, instead of meditating, I sobbed and I couldn't stop. The flood gates had opened and I felt a surge of emotions followed by a strong feeling of love of self that I had never felt before in my life. After the 20 minutes, Trudi, another teacher helping with the weekend, came over to me and gave me a hug. I continued sobbing, saying to her, "I'm worth it. I'm really worth it, and I'm meant to be here (on earth)."

The feeling was supremely powerful. All my feelings of self-hate and worthlessness had left me. I became alive again and felt true to myself for the first time in my adult life. It was the most amazing feeling I have ever felt. It was in that moment that I was able to temporarily release myself from the grip of thinking that "I am my thoughts." I had an experience that I can be separate from my thoughts. I have thoughts, but I am separate from what my thoughts say about me and the world around me. It was liberating. The inner voice that said I was fat, ugly and worthless was still there, but it didn't have a hold over me because I now knew it was just another story being told to me by my ego. I also knew it was ego thinking it was protecting me by keeping me small and hiding in the figurative corner, instead of letting me be my True Self out in the world. The stories and memories were still there, but I was no longer associated as one with those memories, feelings and emotions. I still had them, but I had now become the observer of them. It was freeing. It was a mental liberation!

Something that day just clicked. I leaned into that feeling, a feeling that was telling me to start Imperfection Wellness, a wellness company for the *PERFECTLY* Imperfect. I knew I had to create a wellness program and put these universal truths into a paradigm. I knew without a doubt that the concepts were for everyone, especially those who wanted to get unstuck from the negative and pervasive egoic thoughts they identify with. Everyone has thoughts, and many of these never-ending thoughts of judgment, rating and comparing ourselves to others, often leads us down a road of having negative and overwhelming feelings and emotions. This, in turn, leads us to trying to numb or escape as often as we can to get away from how insecure we feel. Some do this through sex, drugs, alcohol, work, exercise, shopping, eating and other behaviors that allow us to escape from ourselves, and there's no judgment in any of these behaviors. The creation of the paradigm would become my roadmap to wellness, one that I want to share with everyone who may be suffering from association and identification with their thoughts. The paradigm helps people embrace and live life to the fullest, with fulfillment and contentment from within, instead of trying to numb, distract or escape life.

And though I have often been an under-compensator in my life, feeling less than about myself, I also realized this paradigm was for people who are over-compensators, and think they are better than other people. I realized the ego is at play in both scenarios. While my ego said, "You are less than and undeserving," I now know some people's egos say, "You're better than everyone and are entitled to what you want and have."

As I started talking to people about Possley's Paradigm, I realized how many people around me were also struggling. Maybe not as severely as I was, but there was pain. And in talking to people about this, I realized there was no clear and easy way to get help and get unstuck. There was no clear path or plan for people; no roadmap. I knew there wasn't because I had searched for so many years, not finding anything in one place. That is why I think the paradigm is a helpful tool for anyone wishing to come back to Present Moment Living as True Self. It's a tool to getting unstuck so we are no longer feeling better or worse than someone, helping us so we are no longer living with the constant judgments, ratings and comparisons of an ego that is never satisfied and always wanting more. Instead, we can find a way to live with our thoughts, feelings and self-beliefs, knowing we have them, and we are separate from them. Instead of being attached to them or identified as one with them, we are aware of the fact that we have these fleeting thoughts and feelings and our True Self is separate from this egoic voice in our head.

Additionally, I had the realization that mental health & wellness is a human right, and as such, we need to have access to more free and affordable mental health tools and resources. That's why I created the website Imperfection Wellness.com. Many people are suffering and acting out, not because they are bad people, but because they are hurt. This is why the paradigm is here for you and anyone you know. Many who are hurting are identified as one with their ego and the ego's thoughts, feelings and emotions. This book on

Possley's Paradigm is one of many tools to help change that identification and association with our thoughts and self-beliefs. And as we move into discussing the ten universal truths of the paradigm, I hope you find them as helpful as I did on your path to a more centered and fulfilled self.

That night on the balcony in Fire Island was just the beginning. It gave me the strength to continue when I didn't think I had anything left in me. The awakening I had during and after the group meditation was beyond inspirational and carried me forward when I didn't know which way to go. I felt something from outside of me, and it gave me the inspiration to take a leap of faith into the wellness arena, with a goal of helping those who feel lost, broken and hurt like I had for so much of my life.

I still have bad days, but now I know they will pass. Who I am as True Self and how I feel when identified as my ego are two different things. I can feel sad, yet smile. I can feel scared and unsure but move forward, one moment, one step at a time. We are not alone in this, and my goal is that everyone can learn from this inspired paradigm of the ten universal truths laid out here. I still have many negative, ruminating thoughts and false self-beliefs, but now I know how to interact with them differently and its made all the difference in the world!

One candle can light a thousand more candles without ever losing its light. **We are all just like that candle!** We learn to come from an abundance mindset. A mindset that knows there is plenty to go around, just like with the light of that candle.

Scott W Possley

Part II: Ego, Present Moment & True Self

Constantly comparing ourselves to others robs us of the joy of living authentically as True Self in present moment.

Scott W Possley

2

Ego

B efore we go into concepts of the paradigm, I want to explain three concepts that I use frequently throughout the book. They are the concepts of Ego, Present Moment and True Self.

One of the most important concepts to understand in self-healing is the concept of the ego. When I refer to the ego, I am referring to the voice in our head that gives rise to our sense of self; it gives us our identity of who we are. It also gives rise to the concept of me and mine versus them and theirs. This egoic voice also tells us that we are less than or better than someone. It is the voice filled with fear that keeps us small to keep us safe, or over-inflates us to make us feel better than others. When the voice in our head is unobserved and we are unaware of what it is, we falsely believe that we are our thoughts and what those thoughts say about us and the world around us. We listen to that voice which creates self-beliefs that are also self-limiting. When we are in this unobserved state, the ego takes us on a wild roller coaster ride of ups and downs and we often don't know who we really are since we are so connected to this voice.

The ego gives rise to our sense of self and our personal identity. It gives rise to the "I" and "me" within all of us. The ego wants to take care of "me," and wants to make sure "my" needs are met and that "my" things are safe and protected. And when we are identified with or associated as one with the ego without awareness of this, it often means keeping everything for me, while others go without.

I want to be clear that the ego is not bad. The ego is not something we try to conquer or destroy. A healthy ego is a part of us, and throughout this book, I talk of how ego almost destroyed me, but it's not the bad guy here. It was trying to protect me in its own unique way, and I just didn't know how to interact with it, and now I do. I wasn't aware of it and now I am. I didn't know the ruminating thoughts that circled in my head were not from me, but from my ego. This is the distinction we want to make. While I have thoughts, I am not my thoughts. My thoughts are aspects of me, and these thoughts do not define me. When we are not aware of this, our ego can run wild telling us stories about ourselves and others, preventing us from living as True Self in the present moment.

From an evolutionary standpoint, it makes sense that the ego comes from a place of taking care of self first, as this was needed back in the day for self-preservation. However, in today's world of overstimulation from a fear-based 24/7 news cycle and hand-held devices, with alerts and reminders from every corner of our lives, the ego is in overdrive. In a world of judgments and comparisons, the ego of hundreds of thousands of years ago is constantly being bombarded with information of "me and us" versus "them." This can create a sense of fear and worry, a sense of lack, scarcity, and not enough. Our behavior then changes to one of separation, instead of connectedness, so the "I" can have more, while "others" become enemies and may have to go without.

How to Live with the Ego

The ego has always been with us and always will be; therefore, it is not something we fight. It is not something we try to avoid or something we try to destroy. It is not something to overcome. Instead, it is something we become aware of and begin to interact with it differently. It is something we live with because it is a part of us. The ego does serve us in many ways. The ego is protective. It acts as a filter, interpreting and trying to make sense of information from the external world around us, consciously and unconsciously. In turn, this shapes our perceptions of the world as safe or unsafe. Within the interplay of thought and ego is where we have the development of our values, beliefs and self-image, which influences the thoughts we have about ourselves, others, and the world around us.

Through awareness of the ego, we learn to live *with* the ego. We become aware that when we are associated with or identified as one with the ego, we may be missing out on life because we may be living in a fear-based world, filled with worry, anxiety and overwhelm. This manifests in numerous ways, and when left unchecked, it prevents us from living the authentic life we are all born to live.

I like to think of the ego as a hard-working, never-ending commentator, telling us what's right or wrong (often wrongfully so) in the world around us. Learning to live in a healthy relationship with the ego requires us to recognize that the ego is, in part, a commentator constantly scanning the environment for possible dangers. In a 24/7 news cycle with social media's stimulating inputs around every corner, the ego always has something to comment on. This creates a sense of fear, lack, less than or sometimes even an, "I am better than than you" superiority complex based on judgements, ratings and comparisons from the ego.

When any danger is perceived, instantaneously we go into the mode of fight (get ready to attack), flight (running away or escaping the danger), freeze (unable to do anything) or fawn (immediately acting to please in order to avoid any conflict). A surge of hormones is released, like adrenaline and cortisol, and the stress response has been activated. When the saber tooth tiger is about to attack, we need this response in order to survive. In a world where a meeting runs over, our kids need to be picked up and our phones ring and ding on an endless cycle, the ego doesn't know the difference and is now begins to operate in a heightened state as if our survival is *constantly* on the line.

Even when we aren't in this heightened state, the ego is constantly surveying the environment. Living in a healthy relationship with the ego means that we come to realize that the ego loves to use stories, fragments and half-truths as it judges, rates and compares everything going on around us. Many people don't even realize this is even happening. From a rating perspective, things are good, better, best, or bad, worse, and the worst. From a comparison perspective, what he has is better than what they have, or their job is much worse than my job. Additionally, we have the judgment perspective that adds additional layers of how we look down upon or look up to others, based on these stories, judgments, ratings and comparisons. Many of us are always fawning over what someone else has while rarely enjoying the daily riches in our own lives.

While some people have an ego that says they are better than others, when I was stuck in association with my ego's never-ending commentary, I frequently was on the perspective of the losing side and the "less than" side. The egoic voice in my head, through these judgements, ratings and comparisons, said I weighed too much, I wasn't good looking enough and I had no inherent worth or value. I was associated with an egoic commentary that simply wasn't true, but because I was unaware of what I'm describing here, I 100% believed it because it was coming from me.

The commentary was there because the ego was doing what it needed to do, which was keep me safe. And to keep me safe it had to keep me small. In the ego's world, keeping someone small keeps them safe. And in our brain's wiring, even if we feel miserable, it's a comfort we know. Doing something different, such as feeling better about myself, requires an active change on my part, and we will talk through that when we talk about the "Action" step of the paradigm. My association with ego kept me thinking of myself as less than. It kept me small and created a protective shell around me. This shell was a mental nightmare, but it was all I knew. For me, the simplest way to break out of that shell was to drink. When I drank, the ego's commentary disappeared. Sometimes it disappeared for days, but it was always around the corner waiting to pounce.

And it was always so sly. "Go ahead and weigh yourself, I'm sure you didn't gain that much weight." I'd step on the scale and see the number and instantly shrink into emotional nothingness. I'd see a photo of myself and only see ugly. While I knew I had body dysmorphia, with the ego in the driver's seat, I couldn't see anything other than ugly, saying to myself, "that's not dysmorphia, I'm just not a good-looking person. I'll never look like *them*." I would then compare myself to someone who was good looking and see how I didn't measure up. As I was comparing myself, I did what many of us do. I compared my weaknesses to someone else's strengths, and I always came up short.

As the ego's commentary told me I was overweight and ugly, and nobody really liked me, I thought I brought nothing to the table unless I turned on the charm. I would try becoming a funny, joking chameleon, being who I thought others wanted me to be. This caused a cycle of ups and downs, creating an overall feeling of worthlessness.

Many reading this will not have the depths of despair from their egoic thoughts that I had, but few escape the ego unless they've been trained to. From fears of public speaking to being nervous on the first day of work to getting ready to go to a school dance, nerves get all of us. From thinking we are better than someone or some group or that we are not as good as someone else, we've all experienced the ego at play. To me, this is all ego and is the epitome of our association with our ego. To sum this up: If you're thinking about your thinking, you're likely associated with your ego.

I want to underscore that we don't try to escape the ego. That would be futile. Instead, we bring awareness (the first universal truth of the paradigm) to our ego and our experiences. We start to realize we can create some distance from these thoughts and the voice of this never-ending commentator. We realize that in trying to protect us, our ego running wild has separated us from each other, and turned us against each other in some instances. It has told us we are better than others and worse than others, keeping us small or grandiose.

Starting with awareness, we can begin to slowly dissolve our direct association with the ego and begin to appreciate it for what it is, a perception mechanism that is not always based in reality, but instead a perception of our reality based in fragments, stories and half-truths. Through this process of awareness, we realize 99% of what we react to is not a saber-tooth tiger, but a perception of it, and this awareness help us return to the present moment as True Self.

Understanding the Three Ego Archetypes

While the ego is an all-encompassing concept, from my perspective on wellness, I also see it expressed through three primary archetypes observed in my life and the world around me. While these are not scientific or official categories, they help me conceptualize what is driving the egoic voice in my head. I call them the insecure ego, the morality ego, and the narcissistic ego. Each of these is unique but they do have one thing in common, and that is fear.

The insecure ego arises out of fear and says, "You are not enough."; it arises out of attachment saying, "You are nothing without this person. You are nothing unless you have this worldly possession (e.g., the newest car or the fanciest mobile phone on the market)." It arises out of desire saying, "You will only be happy and have self-worth once you attain this job, this job title, this socio-economic status, this body type or way of looking or this 'perfect' partner who will complete you."

For me, this was my "everyday" ego. This ego voice said to me, "You are not enough! You need a better job to be anything, your house isn't good enough, you aren't good enough." This is the cruel ego that I lived with for many years, falsely believing I was what this egoic voice said to me.

The morality ego arises out of fear and adds judgment saying, "Can you believe they did that? I would never do such a thing, and they shouldn't either. I am better than them for my choices and my way of life." It is the voice that casts judgment first and places "me" away from "them" as a protection to preserve self. When a person is in judgment of others, holding themselves in a higher regard, and rarely has all of the facts, it is likely they are associated with their morality ego.

The religious morality ego has done a lot of damage in our world. When foundational religious texts talk of love, and then those so highly associated with their morality ego turn one group of people against another, wars and individual attacks break out, "in the name of God." This has little to do with God and more to do with a morality ego gone unchecked, because we are not even aware of the ego's influence on us. The herd has spoken and the ego wants us to be included, so we go along with what we're told by the mass media and other influential sources. This is not a critique on any religion or any religious beliefs. On the contrary, it is bringing awareness to the fact that we all have a morality ego and when unchecked, it can do great harm to "others" not in "my" group.

The narcissistic ego also arises out of fear, and places the individual far above others, with an inflated sense of their own abilities and achievements. It says to the self, "I am the best and I am much better than you. To make sure I stay in the number one position, I will do anything necessary to keep me here." This is the ego that has an excessive sense of self-importance. It needs admiration from others and constant validation. When a person is associated with this ego, they are still coming from a place of fear and insecurity, but they over-compensate, rationalize, project their fears onto others, or use other defense mechanisms to maintain this false sense of superiority.

Additionally, power and control are guiding forces for those identified with the narcissistic ego. As ego is based in fear and wanting more, we see it manifest by trying to create a common enemy, to protect this grandiose self-image and to ensure that, "I get my way." It's the idea that if we band together against "this group" of people, only then can we protect ourselves from "them," and at times, wanting to win at any cost In reality, there is rarely ever anything to protect people from, but the barrage of grandiose, false statements leads some to follow the narcissist's loud voice, while marginalizing others who have done nothing wrong at all.

Regardless of which type of ego association is dominant with each of us, in general, the ego is also the part of us that laughs when someone we don't like fails. It is the commentator that trolls and leaves nasty anonymous comments online. When someone has a major public temper-tantrum meltdown at the slightest inconvenience, it is likely they are 100% associated with their ego, as they go from a peaceful calm to a violent rage in a split-second.

The ego is the part of us that posts in hopes of getting likes, and then is devastated when we don't get the "magic number" of likes and follows that we secretly hoped for. Association with ego is seen in our politicians and the political media machines on all sides, using us as political pawns to get more votes, as they constantly create an "us vs. them" mentality. In reality, we have much more in common as humans than not, but when we live in ego, we cannot see or feel this and it keeps the "us vs. them" mentality alive at everyone's expense.

The ego's influence can be seen in our 24/7 news cycle filled with the fear of doom, destruction and death, as well as the clear fear messaging we are sent that can sometimes sound like the following: "They are coming to get us. They want to take over, to take your children and ruin your values and all that you hold near and dear in life. They want to take all that you worked hard for." This kind of messaging capitalizes on the ego's fear that we have associated so heavily with. At times we are so unaware of ego that we have started believing opinions as facts, and tall-tale lies and stories as truth, which becomes our perception of reality. When we separate that person from the identification with the ego, we get to the True Self, and there is beauty and goodness there, guaranteed!

When we are stuck associated with ego and egoic thoughts, we may feel less than or falsely believe that there is not enough to go around; that I need more or I need it all, be it money, status, power or possessions. This often leads to health issues, insomnia, anxiety and excessive behaviors to self-medicate or numb ourselves because we are so associated as one with these thoughts. We believe them because we've never been told not to—until now.

We create attachments to job titles and possessions because we falsely think if we have "this title" or "this brand-new expensive item" that we will then be happy. The sad truth is, when we get these items or that job title, eventually the newness wears off and we are still left feeling empty and lost, because the ego is never fulfilled. This leads to another problem often seen in our society. When the fear, anxiety and depression become too much, we turn to drugs, sex, alcohol, overeating, compulsive shopping or exercising and other behaviors to mask, escape, avoid, suppress, and repress how we feel when we are in this association with the false small self, the egoic self. The egoic thoughts that come out of false small self are fragments of stories, inflated and deflated half-truths, and are rarely on point with what happened, is happening or will happen.

The Benefit of Separating from the Ego

By realizing we are separate from our ego and egoic thoughts, we begin to uncover our True Self. And in finding our True Self, we naturally find self-love, peace, tranquility and contentment from within as we come back to the present moment. Fears, anxieties and overwhelm leave or lessen. As our world changes, as we age, as we lose loved ones, as our job/job title changes or as other fleeting externals change, we may feel sad or grieve, which is appropriate and needed, but we are no longer identified as one with these feelings. We become identified as True Self, free of egoic attachment and identification.

We know we will be ok, because when we are identified with our True Self, we are free of the ego's fear-based reality. We enjoy the world around us in present moment, because present moment is all we have. We begin to transcend the feelings of fear, lack/scarcity, anger, pride, etc., and move towards love, contentment, joy and peace. We still have ego, but we are now aware of it. We begin to see how we have identified as one with our ego, and this awareness starts creating space from the ever-needy, ever-fearful ego.

It is estimated that humans have between 6,000 and 60,000+ thoughts a day depending on what literature you read. If those thoughts have commentary from the ego and are a false reality, keeping us out of present moment, then we are constantly living in fear, under the spell of the ego's thirst that will never be quenched. For so many years, I believed my negative, egoic thoughts which fed my feelings, self-beliefs and emotions. I thought to myself, "Well, the thoughts are coming from me, so they must be true, right?"

No, not right! Now I am aware and I know that the thoughts are stories, fragments and half-truths of reality with a never-ending commentary from the ego. Now that I am aware of this, I can separate from my thoughts and come back to present moment. My happiness is not directed by the manipulation of thoughts from my ego, and my association as one with them. I now see the world differently, and live my life differently. I still find myself associated with my thoughts, but now I use the paradigm for getting and staying unstuck from what my ego says about me and the world around me. Now I live with awareness, contentment and fulfillment from within.

Sitting in acceptance of present moment doesn't mean that we we don't engage with the world around us while making intentional choices for tomorrow. It's quite the opposite. It empowers us to engage in life more fully.

Scott W Possley

3

Present Moment

M uch of my life was spent ruminating about the past: "Why did I do that? Why didn't I do this? I should have said this! I should have done that." I also spent a lot of time worrying about the future: "What if this happens? What if that happens? Should I do this or not?" I was so overwhelmed with choices that I didn't know what to do, so I sometimes sat frozen and immobile, struggling to make a simple decision.

Humans have thousands of thoughts each and every day. Many times, our thoughts are pervasive and it's normal to ruminate on these thoughts. To be human is to have thought. I once read, "It's not, 'I think, therefore I am,' but rather, 'I am, therefore I think.'" I loved this because it normalized what was going on inside my brain with these never-ending thoughts. I mention this because when we are tied to pervasive, ruminating thinking, life in the present moment escapes us because we are living in the past or future.

When we are associated as one with these thoughts, always worrying about what's around the corner or living with regrets of the past, we are missing out on the beauty of present moment. All we have is the here and now. Though we can learn from the past, it is over and cannot be changed. Though we strategize and plan for our future, engaging in all of life's choices that are available to us, we are also aware that there are variables outside of our control that will shape tomorrow. The future is an unknown because of these variables that are outside of our control. This doesn't mean we don't engage in the world around us or try. It's the opposite. We now see that there are infinite possibilities available to us, and when things go differently than planned, we will soon learn in Chapter 7 how to sit in acceptance of this.

So often, we are going through the motions of daily life and it's a blur. We are multi-tasking and living in a world of reminders, alerts, e-mails, texts, news, social media and other commitments. We mindlessly scroll social media, sometimes numbing ourselves due to the overwhelm, living vicariously through others. All the while, we end up missing out on what we have right in front of us at this very moment, the endless possibilities of the present moment.

In the past, I have tried living in present moment, but I was always hijacked into the past or future by that egoic voice in my head. The paradigm became the roadmap I needed, bringing me back into the present moment. I still find myself getting pulled into association with ruminating thoughts and belief patterns, living in the past or worrying about the unknown future. The difference now is that I am aware of this tendency and my patterned behavior, and I am able to use the concepts of the paradigm to get unstuck from the voice in my head and return to present moment.

Many of us think we are in the moment and have thousands of photos and videos to prove it, though few will ever be looked at again. We are so focused on capturing present moment for the future that we miss out on the actual moment right before our eyes. I have been to many concerts where I have taken photos and videos throughout the concert. I think it's the best moment ever, and I'm trying to capture the wonder of this moment on a video. I would get home, never look at the photos and videos, only to realize I was so focused on capturing the moment for later that I missed out on the actual present moment experience.

Even when I do look back at my video, the experience is now in the past. While I remember enjoying that song or moment, the wonder and excitement of that present moment I was trying to capture is not in that video. I missed out on an experience in trying to record it for the future. Now when I am at a concert, I keep my phone down and fully immerse myself in the concert, fully immersed in present moment. I am not saying don't capture moments, but I make sure the priority is for me to enjoy the present moment first.

Mindfulness: Life at Half Speed

We will talk more about this in Chapter 13, but one of the easiest ways to return to present moment is by doing any task at half speed. By doing so, you are automatically more mindful about the task at hand; you have to override your default thinking mode and come into present moment when doing something at half speed. The next time you text someone, text them at half speed. The next time you get dressed, dress at half speed. The next time you wash your hands, wash them at half speed.

When was the last time you remember washing your hands? Washing your hands in present moment can be pretty amazing if you give the process your full attention by simply washing them at half speed. Go wash your hands right now. Pay attention to the many steps involved. Washing your hands is not just one step; it is multiple steps. You turn the water on, you adjust the temperature, you get your hands wet and feel the water on your skin, you feel the soap change the feeling of your hands rubbing against each other, you feel how it changes again when the water washes the soap away, you turn the water off, and you dry your hands off. There are likely even more steps involved. When you come out of your default thinking mode into the present moment experience, you begin to transcend these never-ending thoughts, if only for a split-second. That's the space we want to create and over time, that space grows as we continue returning to the present.

When you do any task at half speed, it becomes an experience and it brings you back to the present moment when you pay attention to each and every step. Now try it with making a sandwich and stay in present moment as you are eating it. It's a new experience! When you have this mindfulness mindset with everyday tasks, you bring your awareness into present moment living.

Whatever happened yesterday is over and tomorrow is an unknown, so we sit in the comfort (and often times discomfort) of the now, this very present moment. Over time, we gain an inner peace by letting go of these past regrets and resentments. We improve relationships because we are fully present for them and for the person we are engaging with as opposed to always waiting to jump in with what we want to say instead of listening to what they are telling us.

Present moment is the simplest gift we don't even know we have, within ourselves at all times. Do something today at half speed and be present in the moment, in the experience. Feel what it feels like to be in the here and now. It's magical. And we get to do this each and every day when we separate from our thoughts and worries of the past and future, and are able to come back to this moment.

With present moment living, we are aware life is lived in the here and now. When we choose to live in present moment, we are liberated from the past. We may have learned a valuable lesson from the past, but we don't live in the past. We don't live with regrets and frustrations for what did or didn't happen. We let go of past resentments and regrets, and bring appreciation to this moment we have, sitting in acceptance of how things are in this very moment. It doesn't always mean we like how things are in this moment, but when we sit in acceptance of present moment, we are empowered that in this moment, we can make a change and engage in life today which influences our tomorrow.

Additionally, the future is an unknown. Yes, we can influence tomorrow through planning and our actions, engaging and interacting in our life, knowing it's not a passive process, but we are also aware that we do not have direct control of all of the many variables in the world. This is why we come back to the beauty and tranquility of present moment. We live in the present moment of today, making choices in the realm of today. We are aware that our future will be influenced by these choices, but regardless of the outcome of these choices, our happiness and fulfillment is in the present moment. It is all we have and we cherish it.

The unobserved mind believes what our thoughts say about us, and the price we pay is living as our small self with fear and worry, ruminating on the past and future, as we miss out on present moment. When we transcend ego, we find our True Self there waiting for us to live our lives to their fullest with contentment and fulfillment from within!

Scott W Possley

4

True Self

The True Self is who we ultimately aspire to live as in this world, and this is what this paradigm sets out to help you find. The True Self is separate from the smallness of the ego. When we are identified as one with the ego, we are living as small self. True Self is fulfilled and finds contentment from within. It also realizes, "While I have thoughts, I am separate from those thoughts as they are not the real me, they are not my True Self." As True Self, we can appreciate the many fleeting externals in our lives, such as age, beauty, a job/job title, how big our house is or how nice our car is, etc., *but we are not defined by them.*

When we are aligned and associated with our True Self, instead of as our small, egoic self, we know we are strong, even when we feel weak. We know we can do whatever we set our mind to, even when the odds seem stacked against us. We have our self-worth from within, rather than from an external source, and this gives us an internal strength that isn't taken away by time (aging) or passing worldly possessions because our strength isn't fleeting, it is within us.

True Self is the purest and most sincere form of ourselves. It isn't tainted by societal conditioning, fears, worries and ego-based desires. It lets go of shame and guilt, forgiving self and others. When we are identified as True Self, we have an inner peace, and an understanding that everything will turn out ok. True Self also connects us to something greater than ourselves, whatever that may be, such as God, The Divine, Nature or the Universe. God takes on many connotations for people. Some are drawn towards the word/term/concept, while others withdraw from it. God to me means Source, Spirit, Universe, Nature, Consciousness, The Divine or any other word that works for you that means something bigger than you that is outside of yourself. This is your journey, so define it how you want to. Make it resonate with you!

To find True Self, we have to peel away layers of conditioning, fears and false beliefs to reconnect with an authentic version of ourselves. Because we have never been taught how to do this, and because living authentically is new for many people, we will stumble many times along the path, knowing we can pick ourselves back up and try again. By utilizing the concepts of the paradigm, we begin this journey of uncovering and reconnecting with our authentic True Self!

The false self or small self on the other hand is protected and overseen by the ego as we've discussed. The ego is that voice that warns of impending danger and beats us up for past mistakes. I had been identified as one with small self for so long and I falsely believed that I am my thoughts, feelings and emotions, instead of realizing I have thoughts, feelings and emotions. This is an important distinction.

The Benefit of Recognizing True Self

As I used the paradigm, I brought awareness to my ego and I suddenly realized that while I have thoughts, feelings and emotions, I am separate from them. When I think that I am those thoughts, it can feel like it is unchangeable and it can be easy to become overwhelmed and lose hope. Knowing I am separate from my thoughts, but I have these feelings and emotions, I learn to live with ego and the ego's commentary on life around me. I become the observer of my ego (more about this in Chapter 8) and eventually I am able to smile at the antics of it instead of fighting it. This is truly liberating!

When I realize I merely have these thoughts, feelings and emotions, knowing they are not a part of me, but rather something that I am experiencing, I now know that this thought, feeling or emotion will pass. I can then come back to association with my True Self and return to present moment living. It doesn't mean I don't experience the feelings and emotions. We have our feelings and emotions for a reason and need to deal with them in present moment. We move from, "I am my feeling and emotions" to "I have this feeling or emotion, and it doesn't define me as a person." This allows us to create the space needed for greater awareness—allowing us to enjoy all that is in this present moment. I have a thought, I have a feeling, I have an emotion, and these are fleeting. Once I realize they are fleeting, I come back to my True Self and begin living in the present moment instead of ruminating about the past or future.

Part III: Possley's Paradigm

As we now know, many people are associated with and identify as one with their thoughts, feelings, emotions and self-beliefs, being defined by them instead of realizing that they are mere fleeting aspects of ourselves and that we are separate from them. When we are associated with them, we may be living in the past with regrets, or worried about the future; trying to find happiness in fleeting externals like job titles, our relationship status, how many likes we got on social media and what material goods we possess. We compare ourselves to others, judge ourselves and others and live with constantly changing expectations of what we think life "should" be, as opposed to being in the moment, accepting life as it comes, finding contentment and fulfillment from within. We often feel like we are always coming up short, leading us to miss out on the beauty of the present moment, as we tell ourselves stories made up of fragments and half-truths of information as we emotionally time travel to the past and future.

I created Possley's Paradigm to use as a tool or roadmap to help people get unstuck from identifying as one with these thoughts and self-beliefs; to start questioning our patterned behaviors that we can now change about ourselves so we can live life more authentically and engage intentionally with the world around us. While we learn from the past and plan for the future, we are aware of this instead of mindlessly being pulled in one direction or the other, which leads to us missing out on present moment, the only moment we have. We move away from a mindset of always reacting to our environment to responding and engaging with our environment. The goal is to get unstuck and to stay unstuck from these pervasive, ruminating thoughts/thought patterns instead of living with and being emotionally held hostage by fear, worry and other negative emotions.

When we apply the concepts of the paradigm to our daily lives, we are able to see that we are separate from our thoughts and come back to present moment living. Instead of storytelling and time-traveling, we begin to accept things exactly as they are. It doesn't always mean we like things as they are, but we start with accepting this "is-ness" of life in current state, finding our contentment and fulfillment from within, and bringing intention and strategy to our next right action.

Additionally, we become aware that this is a process. It is not a one and done, read the book and everything is fine. It's about applying the concepts each and every day. We have years of patterned behaviors, self-beliefs, stored stresses, thoughts, worries, fears and anger to unfold. Daily application of one or more of these concepts is what ultimately breaks us free. Print out a copy of the paradigm from ImperfectionWellness.com and apply the concepts when things are going well so you know how to apply them when things aren't going so well.

One of the foundational ideas of the paradigm is, "I am separate from my thoughts." I have thoughts, but I am separate from them. For me, I visualize my thoughts sitting on the left, and the person I am in present moment/in my body, is sitting on the right so to speak. We co-exist, but we are separate. We don't try to stop or fight our thoughts; they will always be there! Instead, we learn how to identify that we are separate from our thoughts so we aren't living associated as one with and identified as our thoughts.

The paradigm is meant to be fluid. It is not, "Follow these nine pillars in this specific order." Instead, learn about these ten universal truths and see which one(s) resonate with you. You may also have additional concepts that are helpful to you from another tradition or worldview. If it's working for you already, don't stop. Just keep building your arsenal of resources.

When you apply the concepts of Possley's Paradigm, you can expect to:

- **Begin living in the present moment** instead of living in the past or future, constantly storytelling/fantasizing about what we could have, or should have said or done. We become aware that present moment is all we have!

- **Find contentment & fulfillment from within**. We begin to understand that we are more than societal labels of what we have, such as what kind of a car we drive, how big our house is or what possessions we own. I call these "fleeting externals." When we are attached to these fleeting externals and find our self-worth in them, when they change, so does our self-worth and happiness. We learn that we can enjoy these things, but our self-worth and happiness are separate from having or acquiring them. These fleeting externals come and go, but our self-worth and contentment are from within. We have this knowledge as our solid foundation.

- **Increase self-confidence & self-worth**. "I am more than what my thoughts say about me and the world around me." What you think of me (whoever "you" are) and what I, myself, think of me, is none of my business, as these are fleeting opinions, a type of thought, based in ego.

- **Begin living with an abundance mindset**, knowing there is plenty to go around. We move away from a mindset of scarcity, lacking or not enough, and move towards a mindset of abundance, knowing there is plenty to go around for all.

- **Start living more authentically in the world**, free of judgments, ratings and comparisons of self and others. We start living in the world instead of trying to escape it through numbing or distracting behaviors such as over-eating, drinking and drugs to name a few of the many numbing behaviors we all have. Note: There is no judgment in any of these behaviors, as I have a long history of over-indulging behaviors that I will talk about in this book. Now that I am aware of why I over-indulged, I realized how I was trying to cope by numbing and trying to escape from the incessant chatter of my egoic thoughts. If any of these behaviors resonate with you, make sure you focus on self-forgiveness and self-compassion as you are working your way through this book. We are fallible humans who make mistakes and the last thing you need to do is beat yourself up over it. Commit each day to doing your best, knowing you may stumble and fall, while also knowing you will get back up as you are doing the work!

Lastly, when we understand and apply the paradigm to our daily lives, we begin to uncover our True Self that has always been there. There are still times when I have bad days, I am frustrated at what "is," or I find myself judging, rating or comparing myself and others. Now that I have the paradigm, I have a roadmap for getting unstuck from all this noise in my head allowing me to live more authentically. The thoughts, feelings, emotions, patterned behaviors and self-beliefs come and go and are they are not who I am, but instead, they are aspects of me that I'm experiencing. When I am aware of this, I am open to the possibility of change.

With this awareness, the emotional pain lessens and I am able to reengage with living life in present moment, with contentment and fulfillment from within. I am able to be the observer of my thoughts. I am able to have two emotions at once, feeling happy while also feeling sad. I am no longer suppressing or repressing my feelings and emotions because I am afraid of or not wanting to feel anything that isn't pleasant. I don't define myself by how I feel, by my patterned behaviors or self-beliefs or what my emotions are, as I know my feelings and emotions frequently change.

Instead of being an angry, sad or depressed person, I am a person who has these feelings and emotions or is feeling anger. Our thoughts, feelings, emotions, self-beliefs and patterned behaviors no longer define us, but are aspects of us. When we realize this, we can come back to living in the present moment, the only moment we truly have, allowing our True Self to shine.

I am more than what my thoughts say about me
and the world around me!

Scott W Possley

5

Awareness

Awareness is the first step in our awakening, so we are no longer passively sleepwalking through life.

A wareness is the starting point of the paradigm because so much hinges on being aware of what is going on with ourselves and our perception of the world around us. With awareness, we understand that we have thousands of thoughts each day, as all humans do, and we always will. We begin to understand that the ego gives endless commentary on these thoughts, knowing that this commentary is based in fear and not based in reality. This causes some people to overcompensate, feeling superior to others, while others undercompensate, feeling inferior to others. We also become aware that we inadvertently become attached to and connected with these thoughts, as if they are a part of us; as if we are one with them.

This is a fallacy and we learn that we are separate from these thoughts. We have them, but they are not who we are, and we are not what these thoughts say about us and the world around us. These thoughts have no intrinsic meaning in and of themselves. All meaning we give to our thoughts is created by us, with most of our thoughts being fragments, stories, half-truths and interpretations of the past or future.

To be alive is to have thought. I always labeled myself as an over-thinker, when in reality, I was a normal everyday human who has thousands of thoughts each and every day. The difference was, I inadvertently became attached to my thoughts and identified as one with them, falsely believing I was what my thoughts said about me and the world around me. And I want to make a clear distinction from intentional thinking or rational thought, where we are bringing intention to thought for planning purposes, such as studying for a test or planning a trip. There is no problem with this. The problem is with the random, mindless mental chatter we all have. The chatter that says, "I'm less than or better than someone," the chatter that keeps us up at night and the never-ending chatter that overwhelms us with regrets of the past or worries about the future.

When we recognize our relationship to our thoughts, we know that the thoughts are there, that they always will be there and we don't try to fight them. We also don't try to have control over them. This would be futile. Instead, we learn how to separate from our thoughts by first bringing awareness to this idea that we have thousands of thoughts every day and then we become separate from them by observing them. We will talk more about how to be the observer in Chapter 8.

Our pervasive, ruminating thoughts have endless commentary from our ego, and association with our ego keeps us associated with our small self or false self. The false self is a version of us that does not feel inner-fulfillment, and lives in fear, giving rise to feelings of worry, sadness, anger and envy to name a few. The small egoic self never has enough and will go to great extremes to get what it thinks it needs.

The ego creates separation from others by defining self as number one. In pre-historic days, this was necessary and self-protective, but left unchecked without awareness, it can also be self-destructive. The goal is not to destroy the ego, but to be aware that it is there and to live with it. The ego is not going away and its intentions are to be helpful in our daily lives. However, when the ego is left unchecked, it can lead to association with its negative thought patterns and take us to extreme highs and lows.

Though we are separate from our thoughts, many of us identify as one with them. If my thoughts say that I am less than or more than someone, and I believe the thought and have associated with the thought, then I believe that I am less than or more than, when in reality I am equal to that person. Additionally, when we identify as one with these thoughts, we are rarely in present moment. We are living in the past and future, believing our egoic fearful thoughts. This create stress, anxiety, depression and a myriad of other emotions and physical ailments, taking us out of the beauty that is present moment living.

An example of this happened to me one day when I was on the beach for my early morning walk. The beach is always a place that gives me peace, joy and tranquility. Present moment for me that day was beautiful. The sun was rising over the horizon, the beach was quiet and pretty empty except a small group off to the side playing. There was a gentle breeze and birds were frolicking in the distance. It was a gorgeous scene with the waves gently crashing as the tide was coming in. It was serene and peaceful. I was in my element. Suddenly, those thoughts, that inner voice I had associated with over the years, started becoming louder and meaner. Before I knew it, I was associated as one with these thoughts, and believed what they were saying. The thoughts were just cruel!

"God you're pathetic. You're ugly, overweight and don't have any friends that really care about you. You're single and can't hold down a relationship. What's wrong with you? There's obviously something wrong with you. How embarrassing! You don't have the beach body that everyone else has. You're so out of shape...look at you! You should be embarrassed. Ah nice, look at the group of people playing on the beach. That's something you'll never have. Just keep pretending, fool." The thoughts weren't always this bad, but this day they were pretty severe. These ruminating thoughts multiplied and continued, pulling me down because I believed what they said about me, not having the awareness of what was going on in this moment.

I left the beach heavily identified with the thoughts swirling in my head. The beautiful beach moment was destroyed. This led me to feel defeated, deflated, depressed, overwhelmed and broken. I went back to the house to get ready for the day. And as I was already associated with my thoughts, when I looked in the mirror, all I saw was an ugly pathetic person looking back at me. This wasn't true of course, but it was me believing the egoic commentary. I'd avoid mirrors and photos at all costs, because all I would see is an ugly person staring back. My thoughts said I was ugly and worthless, so it must be true! It's coming from me!

The friends I was in the beach house with were ready and we would finally go back to the beach as a group. Even though I was there with friends who cared about me, I minimized it. My inner voice had already told me that morning that I wasn't worth anything. It said I wasn't like my friends and that I was a pitiful outcast and didn't belong.

I always felt like I was on the outside looking in. I'd try to talk or tell a story, but no matter what the response, that inner voice said, "SHUT UP! No one wants to hear from you," and I would cower and try to use humor and alcohol in hopes of trying to fit in since I didn't feel like I belonged. I was living in shame and embarrassment because I falsely believed what these horrible thoughts said about me. I didn't know that I was separate from them, let alone how to separate from my identification with them. By becoming aware of my egoic thought patterns, I realized I could interact differently with these never-ending thoughts and commentary from my fear-based ego.

There were often times, outside of this beach experience, when I would be out and about enjoying life and the thoughts wouldn't be as menacing, but sooner or later, the inner-saboteur would arrive and make sure I was put back in my place!

I often asked myself why would the ego do this? Why would it self-sabotage me in such a way? I came to the conclusion that by keeping me small, it created a protective layer around me that was almost impenetrable. I would shut down, shut off and push people away. I didn't want to do that. I wanted the exact opposite. But in keeping me small, the ego was doing what it thought was right. It was trying to protect me.

The ego can work on the flip side for someone who is grandiose and thinks they are better than everyone. The person with grandiose thoughts of self, thinking they are better than and above others, still has a fear-based ego association. The difference is that this type of person over-compensates to feel safe and invincible and the ego is trying to protect them too.

Lastly, it is a rare gem to come across a person associated as True Self, who takes life as it is, day by day in present moment. This person is aware of the ego's chatter and bring intention and awareness to their thoughts. When associated as True Self, we live in and enjoy the bliss of what "is" in this world. True Self accepts what is in life. When associated as True Self, we have happiness from within and an inner-fulfillment, and are better able to weather the storm of daily living, knowing "this too shall pass." This is the experience we all have available to us by simply letting go of our attachment to our egoic thoughts, and it all starts with awareness.

I've seen people close to me who inadvertently choose to live in chaos. Through this chaos, they don't have to stop and think. They don't have to be alone with themselves. For the longest time, the moment I walked into my apartment, I turned on the TV to have background noise. The idea of silence was crippling to me. The isolation of living by myself was overwhelming to me because I didn't like who I was due to believing the commentary of my ego. I would fill space with mindless online shopping, binging TV and drinking. I had a lot of hobbies to pass the time as well. These hobbies were healthier so to speak, but in hindsight I realize the activities were there to fill the void of the silence I never wanted to sit in. Now that I practice the paradigm, meditate daily and teach meditation, sitting in silence isn't something I fear. I am able to better cope with what "is" in the world around me as I sit with acceptance. I still have bad days, but I know "this too shall pass" and I am better able to cope.

Filling the void and numbing can take many forms and may include exercise, shopping, cooking/baking, alcohol, drugs, sex, or binging on TV for hours on end (one of my favorites). There is zero judgment in any of these activities, whether they are done in moderation or excess. As we change our relationship with our thoughts and move into becoming aware of our them, we want to avoid labeling, judging, rating or comparing, as this would be the ego returning. We simply want to understand if our behavior is masking or helping us to escape something else. If it is, then we bring awareness to it.

We also show empathy to ourselves. We treat ourselves as we'd treat a loved one or beloved pet. Once I became aware of my actions and why I was doing them, I was initially hard on myself, beating myself up and reliving past experiences through a lens of critique and judgmental. Over time, as I continued utilizing the other steps in the paradigm, I was able to be more supportive, kinder and more empathetic to myself.

When I was so heavily associated with my thoughts, living in my head, I was missing out on the beauty and wonder of present moment. I had no awareness at the time so I didn't know any better. Your version may be quite different, being more or less intense, but if you have a thought and are heavily associated with it, feeling bad about yourself for it, or are thinking about your thinking, then you are likely identified as one with your egoic thoughts. The thoughts may say you are the best person in the world or the worst person in the world. Either way, if you are associated with these extreme thoughts of being better than or worse than others, sitting in judgment with comparisons and ratings, then it is very likely you are associated with your egoic false self.

Through this awareness, we start living separately from our thoughts, knowing that we will always have them, and then we come back to enjoy the beauty of present moment. I'll often say to myself, "I am aware of my thoughts and I am aware that I am separate from them. I am aware they are half-truths and fragments with commentary from the ego, filled with judgments, ratings and comparisons. I choose to align with my True Self instead." Through awareness, as we separate from identification with our thoughts, we start to create a space, however small it may be. It is in this space where our authentic True Self lives, free of worry and overwhelm and anger and jealousy. This is the space we grow overtime when we utilize the paradigm daily.

When left unchecked, the ego can create a dictatorial narcissist or a shell of a person. Many people live between these two extremes. Egoic thinking unchecked leaves you easily manipulated and swayed by emotions. The ego comes from a place of lack, of there being not enough, and a place of scarcity. Even when there is plenty, when there is abundance, such as with wealth and food, the ego says, "Self first. This is mine, and I want it all". This is why we come back to awareness. We become aware that we will always have these thoughts, and instead of resisting or fighting them, we are aware that we can be separate from our ego and can live harmoniously with ego and the ego's commentary on everything in the world around us.

Bringing Awareness into Your Daily Life

Become aware that you are separate from the many thoughts you have each and every day, knowing that you are more than what these thoughts, feelings, emotions and self-beliefs say about you and the world around you.

Become aware that present moment is all we have. Yesterday is over, tomorrow is in the future and largely an unknown.

Bring awareness to present moment by breathing in for a count of four, holding the breath for a count of four, exhaling for a count of four, and holding the bottom of the exhale for a count of four. You automatically come back to present moment when you focus on your inhale and exhale by counting and breathing. This technique is called box breathing and it helps separate yourself from your thoughts, if only for a moment.

Practice some of these awareness statements (or write your own) as part of a daily practice:

- I am aware that I have thousands of thoughts a day and I always will. This is a normal part of being a human. I am aware that I cannot stop or change my thoughts, but I can change how I associate with them (more on this in Chapter 8).

- I am aware that when I am associated or identified with my thoughts, I am likely living in the past or future instead of living in present moment.

- I am aware that these thoughts are fragments and are over/under exaggerations of my experiences or what I wish my experiences were or would be, like fantasy storytelling of the past and future.

- I am aware that these thoughts ruminate or circle repeatedly in our brains, and sometimes we attach ourselves to the thoughts, identifying as one with the thoughts.

- I am aware that I have habituated thought patterns and self-beliefs. I know I can utilize the concepts in Possley's Paradigm to change my association with these thoughts and beliefs over time.

- I start saying to myself, "I *feel* angry (or other emotion)" instead of "I *am* angry," noting that we allow the emotion but we are not defined by the emotion.

- I am aware that my thoughts are likely telling me a false or biased narrative, a story about what the truth really is in a given situation.

- I am aware that these thoughts feel real/feel like the real me, but I am aware they are separate from me.

- I am aware that my ego enjoys storytelling with never-ending commentary. It is storytelling with exaggerated details about the past or future and what I should have done or would do. I am aware this commentary adds additional layers with judgments, ratings and comparisons.

- I am aware that many of my thoughts have no meaning in and of themselves, other than being a part of the ego's commentary.

I am now aware that I am more than what my thoughts say about me and the world around me!

6

Attachment

My self-worth is inherent to me, separate from any attachments I may have.

Have you ever lost something sentimental and felt devastated, or felt better about yourself after buying something extravagant or maybe even defined yourself by or felt a boost in your self-worth based on a job title or the price you paid for something? If so, you're not alone. Chances are you have allowed your inherent self-worth to be defined by something external to you.

Sometimes we even define our worth by a skill we have, something we can do better than someone else. There is nothing wrong with working hard to attain the skill, but our value isn't based on this skill. Often time we even compare what we can't do to what someone can do. We will always come up short, comparing our lowlight reel to someone's highlight reel, when we are looking for things external to us to give us our value and worth.

This is normal human behavior, but when left unchecked, we can find ourselves on an emotional rollercoaster, rising and falling with whatever we've attached ourselves to, all the while not realizing our self-worth is inherent to us. When we become aware of this, we can get off the emotional rollercoaster and find our contentment and fulfillment from within.

In this chapter, when I refer to attachment, specifically egoic, emotional attachment, I am referring to the idea that our self-worth is tied to things outside of us instead of finding it inherently within ourselves. It's when we feel our self-worth only when we are validated by others or we validate ourselves based on our looks, our job title, our salary, the house we live in or the possessions we have. We can even define our self-worth by those around us, be it our partner or friends. For example, having a trophy spouse or friend. There is nothing wrong with having a spouse or friend you want to show off, but your self-worth has nothing to do with this person.

Attachment is not inherently wrong. Look at the healthy attachment of a loving parent to their newborn baby. This is needed for the healthy development of the child. Egoic attachment, on the other hand, is when we are not aware of our attachments and how they subconsciously dictate our self-worth, as well as our happiness, contentment and fulfillment.

The issue arises when we define ourselves based on these external attachments. Without being aware of this, when we lose our trophies, when our beauty fades or we age or we lose our job, or don't have our nice house in the best neighborhood, we end up feeling lost and our self-worth takes a hit. Additionally, our self-worth and contentment fluctuate based on what we do or don't have. Our contentment, fulfillment and happiness lie outside of us, instead of being within us.

Our attachments can sometimes lead to the false belief that our self-worth, happiness or fulfillment in life is solely dependent on things in our external world—these attachments. That person, possession or physical characteristic becomes a part of how we define ourselves, and we have a subconscious false belief that if we were to lose these items or attributes, then we are nothing. Instead of appreciating what we have and not defining ourselves by it, we assign our self-worth or happiness to it.

We may feel lost or find ourselves grasping for our youth or material objects to feel fulfilled, instead of bringing our awareness to the idea that we have inherent worth, something many of us do not realize and have never been told. Starting with awareness, we begin to find contentment and fulfillment from within. We stop chasing happiness as a destination, a destination that will never be reached.

Let's say we have an attachment to an expensive item we purchased. We worked hard and saved up for this item and now we are glad that we have it. We may become so attached to our possession that it becomes a part of our identity, e.g. Now I have worth and I value myself more because of this possession—or even things like my job title, the neighborhood I live in, the size of my house and the things I own.

Through the lens of awareness, we realize these items are not who we are, but merely what we have. We can enjoy what we have, but we become aware that we are not defined by them nor are we better than others because we have them. And while we may become saddened when our new shiny object breaks or is damaged, with awareness of this, we realize we are still the same person we have always been, with or without that item. When we are defined by it and it loses its bright shiny exterior, we feel like we are also tarnished, unless we get a newer, bigger and shinier object, and this is simply not true.

Some of my attachment issues stem from being gay. Even though I had a loving family and great friends, I hid who I was for 20 years, not knowing if they would accept me once I came out. I was never an authentic version of me for fear of rejection, so I became emotionally over-attached to external things to bring me my happiness. I held my attachments tightly and let them define me and my self-worth. My self-worth was outside of me in the fleeting external world which was outside of my control. I was defined by my attachments without realizing it.

This realization came to me in my later adult years. One day I realized how my self-worth was attached to what items I owned, who liked me or who my friends were, what my job title was, how much I made and where I lived to name a few. As I sat there contemplating my many attachments, my eyes filled with tears. I realized I had quite an impressive list of attachments which were fine in and of themselves, but they didn't define my inherent worth at the end of the day. I knew I needed to shift my awareness from, "this defines me," to "I have these things and can enjoy them, but my worth is from within. It always has been and always will be!"

The fear of loss and overwhelm I had a losing these fleeting externals was so intense before I became aware of this concept. Because of this, I searched for approval from others to find my self-worth. And when the fleeting external items and other's approval left or changed, then I was back to feeling lost as I didn't know how to define myself because it was coming from outside of me. It was paralyzing at times.

We also have emotional attachments. This is the sentimental part of us that holds onto objects and people and ideas for a multitude of reasons. I have items from family and friends or I have a belief in something due to how a loved one felt and I hold onto these for dear life. If the item breaks, I'm devastated. I can't imagine parting with it. Or there's a stance or view that a beloved grandparent had that I mirror to show my love and connection to them. Emotional attachments can manifest in a myriad of ways. There is nothing wrong with these connections. What we want to do is to bring our awareness to our emotional attachments, just like with egoic attachments, and realize these attachments do not define us. I can enjoy the keepsake item, but if I part with it or it breaks, it doesn't break the bond I had.

I had a ring from my mom and dad. It was sentimental and something that made me think of them every time I wore it. After moving from one apartment to another, I realized the ring was gone. At first I was devastated! This ring meant so much to me. And it wasn't the actual value, it was the sentimental value I had attached to the ring. After sitting in acceptance that the ring was gone, and becoming aware of the emotional attachment I had with the ring, I suddenly realized the love I had of my parents was no different with or without the ring. The ring was a symbol, one that I cherished, but now that it was gone, I still have a deep emotional connection and love with them. It's not erased because the ring is gone. And I can get a new ring and re-symbolize that ring as a reminder.

Sitting in acceptance of this doesn't mean I like what happened, but I can shift my perspective and realize the emotional attachment to the ring. Awareness of this lessens the pain, and I was able to move on, knowing the actual connection to my parents hadn't changed at all. Do I still enjoy trinkets from the past? Absolutely! But now they don't have the same emotional attachment because I realize they are symbolic and a representation, but not actual connection to what I was holding onto.

Often we have views or mannerisms that we hold onto and can't imagine when someone else feels differently. "How could you feel that way? My grandma always said (insert statement)." We hold onto these emotional connections for dear life sometimes to the point of figurative suffocation to honor our loved one. Again, there is nothing wrong with that. However, through the lens of awareness, we can begin to release the suffocating hold and come back to present moment with a sense of calm and comfort of appreciating what they appreciated, but knowing it's ok that others, including ourselves sometimes, may feel differently.

I also realized my emotional attachments to political beliefs and causes. If someone had an opposing view or diminished something I believed in, I took it as a personal attack. I think this is going on so frequently in our daily lives that we don't even realize it. The political environment and a 24/7 news cycle leave us feeling like everyone is against us. The fear and righteousness of the activated ego come out ready to fight anyone who sees it differently than us.

This is related to egoic attachment in that if my view differed from someone I had on a albeit false pedestal, I didn't know what to do. Was I wrong in my belief if it differed? Or do I lash out and demonize them for having an alternative belief. It may be a stretch, but I came to realize egoic attachment to ideas and beliefs also play a part in how we define our worth and values when it comes to the ego.

My ego loved the soapbox I could get on as I judged, rated and compared my attachment to a stance, thought or opinion the "opposing" side had. It became the sword I would die on each and every time. The emotional toll it took on me wasn't making any difference and I was only hurting myself by being so filled with anger and rage. I came to realize that this initially fueled me and I enjoyed the rush of getting on a political soap box. I was attached to the demonization of anyone from the other side not having my views. It was almost like an addictive drug.

Now that I am aware of attachment, it lessens my emotional connection to everything, including my views and opinions of the world we live in. I still have many of my same views, but the vitriol and anger and soap boxing aren't there. The intensity lessened and now I am able to come to a middle ground. I can have a discussions and meet people where they are, giving me a better chance of influencing change versus yelling at someone or creating an inciting social media post.

There is nothing wrong with my views or someone's opposing views. When I bring awareness to this, it lessens the toxic emotions behind it that only end up hurting me and leaving me emotionally exhausted. I still have my causes, but now I work for something instead of fighting against something.

Bringing Awareness to our Attachments

The first step to changing the effect egoic and emotional attachments have on us is to bring awareness to the attachment. Think of something you are attached to that gives you a sense of worth, something outside of you. Write it down. Look at it. Observe it through the eyes of awareness. Where did it come from? Is it something you have that you enjoy? Or is it something that defines you? Age and body image and beauty are external characteristics that many people struggle with, because we live in a society that values us based on what we look like. Does this apply to you? What if we could change this through the lens of awareness? What if we sit in this discomfort and lean into it (more on this in chapter 10)?

By asking ourselves any number of similar questions, we start to realize we may be attached to a possession, or a physical characteristic about ourselves that positively or negatively affects our perception of an external self-worth. Then we bring our awareness to this, recenter ourselves, and know that our value and worth is inherent, from within ourselves, and that we are enough just in being who we are in the here and now.

We realize we are more than our self-beliefs, thoughts and possessions. Through awareness and our questioning, we begin to realize we can view ourselves as beautiful, enjoy the new car or job title, but our worth and our happiness don't depend on it because these things all change. Our worth isn't centered around it.

Extreme attachment to our self-worth and happiness outside of ourselves is the action of the ego. As we are not taught to distinguish between True Self and egoic small self, we often gravitate towards attachment without realizing it. The price tag that goes along with maintaining this is sometimes too expensive. We live with fear, worry, depression, stress, and anxiety for fear of losing our precious external commodities, fearing what we will be if we end up without them.

The ego's herd mentality protected us thousands of years ago, and while survival mechanisms are necessary (e.g. trust your gut, something feels off), in a 24/7 news cycle motivated by fear and shame, we are no longer in a place to trust these instincts if the ego has taken over. We short circuit at times. And when we are not aware of our attachments, the ego grows while keeping us small and fearful, keeping us under its spell. As I discussed earlier, we do not fight the ego or try to kill the ego. Instead, we become aware of the ego, the egoic thoughts and the egoic attachments, which are based in small self. We will learn in future chapters how to transcend or go beyond the ego, knowing it is always with us.

All this being said, do I enjoy a new car, new clothes, a well-paying job, while living in a nice house or apartment? Yes. That is not on the table to be judged. This is perfectly fine. The difference is none of these things define me. We want to be aware when the attachment takes over and the fear-based ego is not in check. Left to its own vices, it can create an insatiable hunger that is not able to be filled and leaves you feeling empty due to a fear of losing said item.

One time I was traveling by train, and I left my bags on the luggage shelf at the back of the car. Due to an error in reading my ticket, I was in the wrong train car and had to move back one car. This was after the train had left the station, so there was no space for my luggage in the new car and I had to leave my luggage where it was. About 20 minutes into the trip, my egoic thoughts took over and my beautiful train ride was now filled with visions of my bag being stolen. The beautiful 3-hour journey by train was now filled with fear-based thoughts of overwhelming loss, partially due to the attachment I had with my luggage. I saw everyone with their luggage in their line of sight, and even checked on my baggage twice during the journey. While my bag could have been stolen, the chances were in my favor that it would be fine. Simple concern was not what I felt. I had irrational feelings so severe that it altered how I enjoyed the entire train ride.

Finally, I was able to bring awareness to this situation, and it was such a wonderful experience to have. After about two hours, I suddenly started laughing at myself. The most important documents, my wallet, ID, passport, phone and laptop, were with me. What I was stressing about to have in my possession or in my visual sight was a backpack of clothing and personal items, all easily replaceable. The idea of losing these items was so strong that it sent me into a spiral of worry and misery, and it was not worth the emotional toll it took on me. This was an unhealthy attachment for me, and once I realized it, I was then able to enjoy the rest of the train ride. While it wasn't about my self-worth, it was about the overwhelming fear of what would happen if I lost these material goods which were easily replaceable.

Now, do I want to have to replace the clothing and items I had for my trip? No. But the attachment was beyond that. The emotional attachment wasn't about the value or replacing the items. It put all its value on the "my" aspect of the possessions, which were all easily replaceable, albeit inconvenient, had I needed to. This is what I want to call out, the irrational fear due to attachment. My attachment to my items changed the entire train ride into one of unsettled stress—revving up stress hormones in my body that have a much worse effect on my body than having to replace some items. Since I wasn't aware of the attachment initially, I was easily willing to let this all take place. Once I got my luggage and got off the train, I could still feel remnant stress in my body from those first couple hours on the train for the next several hours. And becoming aware of this doesn't mean it won't happen again. It means we will have an understanding of attachment and will be able to catch ourselves quicker the next time.

Now that we are aware of our egoic thoughts and attachments, the challenge is becoming aware in the moment or as close to the moment as possible. This will happen in time. I have been doing this work for many years and still the insidious ego finds a way to sneak in and take over without me realizing it. The ego sits idly by in the corner watching and waiting. It is just as aware that you have learned awareness, so now it has to be a bit more sly about coming out and taking over. On that train ride, the ego found the perfect moment. It saw my attachment to my luggage and the fear of loss I felt and instantly went back to doing what it does best. It created hundreds, sometimes thousands, of scenarios of what could, would or might happen. And none of the scenarios came true, but the stress of the fake scenarios caused me undue stress and ruined a perfectly beautiful train ride through the country.

The simplest solution to counteract this is to bring awareness to the ego and our egoic attachments. We are aware that the ego is a part of us, but we are separate from the ego. When we do this, we create space from the ego, and this space is where the magic of everyday living can occur!

I frequently say to my ego, my egoic thoughts and that egoic voice, "I see you; I am aware that you are an aspect of me—and, I am separate from you. We are in this together, and it's going to be ok. There is no cause to have a fight or flight response right now." I say this to myself to help create space away from the stress response I am so used to having. I continue to build on this day by day, experience by experience. Early on, you may not realize the ego's effect on you until after the fact, and that's ok. Eventually, you will realize it in the moment. This will take time, so take it easy on yourself.

To help me with my awareness of ego, I created a visual for my ego. I call him Tasmanian Scottie, or Taz Scottie for short. Taz Scottie is a beast at times. When I picture him and visualize him as my ego, out to get me and take over, he is panting heavily, and his teeth are sharp as razors. He's about a foot or so tall (he thinks he's taller of course, he's ego), and when he strikes, he's vicious.

During my visualizations of him, he has attacked me and eaten limbs off of my body. He has bitten and scratched my face to the point of trying to destroy me, and I instantly regenerate back to my True Self. When I am True Self, I am indestructible to the ego. Just like I cannot destroy him, he cannot destroy me. When he is in a fit of rage, waging an all-out attack on me, I sit calmly and comfortably and smile, taking slow deep breaths through any discomfort. I hug him and let him know I love him (since he is an aspect of me, and I want to send love), and he continues to try to destroy me until he finally gives in and we are embracing.

The first time I did this visualization exercise, I burst into tears. As I mentally hugged him, he went from Tas Scottie to a scared, crocodile teared version of me from when I was a child. I realized in that moment that Taz Scottie was really a younger version of me. He was scared and filled with fear and anger and rage. When I saw my younger self as ego, I was cowering in a corner. It was literally how I felt as a child and this is how it emotionally plays out as an adult.

In real life, I put on my emotional armor and pretended to be strong and fierce, but on the inside, I was scared, little Scottie, about 5 years old. Now that I could visualize him, it was no longer a fight. We were one and I held onto Taz Scottie without judgment, just pure unconditional love. It was a surreal experience to tell him he is loved unconditionally and that we are in this together. He still acts out, but now I am onto his games and I have become the observer as opposed to being a victim of my own ego.

In the story of the train ride with my luggage, neither 5-year-old Scottie nor Taz Scottie was there. Instead, they morphed into egoic thought. They were thoughts in my mind that I identified as one with, and they were wreaking havoc with my lost semblance of calm, fearing my luggage would be stolen. And even when I knew I was no longer associating with my True Self, but with small self of ego and egoic thought, the attachment was too great to fully overcome in the 3-hour journey. As I said, it did subside eventually. The next day I was back in full awareness of the beauty and grandeur of my True Self, but it still created an immense amount of stress on my body that I'd never wish on anyone.

The lesson learned from this story is that we may not always be aware that the ego has crept in and taken over until after we've taken the bait and reacted. Then in hindsight after we've cooled off, we realize what happened. Over time as we practice this, we will start to realize closer to the actual moment that ego has taken over. Now I am able call it out as it's happening. I am aware as it is happening and I know I need to do one of the action steps that we will talk about in Chapter 13 when we talk about the concept of Next Right Action.

For now, we focus on awareness that we slipped into ego identification and are likely not our rational selves. We know we are not feeling the bliss of True Self and we are ok with this. We do not fight our ego, but merely acknowledge it, while becoming aware of our own level of attachment.

A version of this story will happen again for me. Merely being aware and knowing of our attachment doesn't make it disappear, but it will lessen the emotional stress response we have over time. Each time it happens, the intensity lessens. This is not discouraging at all. In fact, it is quite liberating to know that we are not broken, we will continue to get better, and this too shall pass. And it is great to know that this is part of our humanness that we can overcome and live with, again, finding our contentment and self-worth from within.

Awareness as the first step in relinquishing egoic
and emotional attachments:

Make a list of the attachments you have where the idea of losing them causes fear or upset. Or think of something external that currently defines your self-worth, and then consider what if your worth was inherent, and these externals didn't matter? Sit with this for a moment and simply bring awareness to the concept. If you have any discomfort, take a few slow deep breaths or get up and go for a walk or do another activity, being mindful of what you're doing.

Additionally, ask yourself if you have attachments to a way of thinking, to a way of living, to a way of reacting? Do you have attachment to feeling small? Do you have an attachment to a person, thing or idea?

Do you have attachment to strong negative thoughts of self? And ask yourself, "Am I gaining something by staying small?" What would happen if I came into living as True Self and relinquished these fears?

Keep your awareness on one of your attachments, breathing in and out as you say to yourself:

"My fulfillment and worth comes from within. I am releasing these strong emotional attachments to (insert what you are attached to).

"I sit with the discomfort of any fears I have, knowing the ego gives false comfort to staying small, to staying in fear. I know I will be ok releasing attachment to anything that keeps me small.

"I relinquish attachment to my possessions. I can have the possessions and enjoy them, but they do not define me. I am more than my possessions. My self-worth is inherent and comes from within, not from what I have.

"I relinquish attachment to social status items, be it a job title, the house I live in, the car I drive or the clothes I wear. These are all fleeting externals that are meaningless in and of themselves. I can enjoy these things, but I am aware that my true identity is not tied to them. I can enjoy them and if and when they fade, I am not affected by it."

When it comes to the people we know and love in our lives, relinquishing attachment can be a challenge to think about. People may disagree with what I am about to say when it comes to loved ones, and that is fine, but I also believe we can have unhealthy attachment to people in our lives; defining our intrinsic value and self-worth based on who is in our life.

Recall in the beginning of this chapter when I said attachment can be healthy and is needed for healthy psychological development in human relationships. There is nothing wrong with loving people. The caution flag is waved when we define ourselves, our worth and our inner-contentment by these relationships. It doesn't mean we don't feel emotional pain when people in our lives are hurting or that we don't grieve the loss of a loved one. That is part of love.

For me, and for the purposes of the paradigm, I think of my "over-attachments" to some people in how I used to define myself and my worth based on certain relationships. The attachments I had led to a gut-wrenching paralyzing fear of mine of the thought of losing a loved one or friend. The thought or idea of losing them was so severe, that if that person died, I believed I would be devastated to the point that I couldn't cope or function or go on, that I would be nothing without them here. Yes of course I would grieve, but the paralyzing fear was more than just grief, it was a paralyzing anticipatory grief. This has been something I have dealt with since being a young child and it's crippled me at times. I share here in case this resonates with you. This may not be applicable to you, but if it is, you can say to yourself something similar to below. If what is written below doesn't apply or doesn't resonate, please disregard.

"I relinquish attachment to (name a person). While I love this person, who I am as a person is independent of my relationship with them. I am complete in and of myself, knowing this person accentuates me but in no way are they able to complete me, as I am fully complete in and of myself. Relinquishing over-attachment to someone doesn't mean I don't love them or enjoy them or do things for them, but I am letting go of the emotional fear of losing them or being defined by them, while still enjoying their company. My life will not end if something happens to them and when they do die someday, as we all do, I will grieve and a part of me will feel the loss, but I know they are still with me and I can move on day by day, knowing their spirit is always with me and guiding me.

7

Acceptance

Acceptance doesn't mean I have to like what is, was, or will be—but I choose to sit in acceptance, embracing the 'is-ness' of life rather than constantly fighting it.

A cceptance is the act of embracing present moment exactly as it is, accepting the past exactly as it was, and accepting the future, exactly as it will be. Acceptance is one of the challenges I still have in my daily life. It is something I continue to work through, because the egoic voice will always have a want, desire or opinion on how yesterday "should" have gone and how today and tomorrow "should" go. The egoic voice within leads us to believe that we can control the world around us, when I am here to shed light on the realization that we may influence the world around us, but we cannot control much of anything, other than ourselves and how we respond.

With this awareness, we begin accepting the "is-ness" of life, with all of its ups, downs, twists and turns. It is accepting the cold, dark and stormy day as much as the warm, sunny, summer day. It is accepting working at an unfulfilling job and having a challenging boss and choosing to stay versus choosing to find a new job. It is accepting being single and enjoying the current car I have instead of saying I will only be happy when I have a partner, a new car or a new job. We accept life exactly as it is today, because when the new car or job happens, shortly after the honeymoon period ends, the unfulfillment will soon return if we are looking for fulfillment outside of ourselves.

The same goes with our bodies and our age. It's accepting my body today exactly where it is, with wrinkles, gray hair, my skin color, my hair texture, and a myriad of other characteristics we think we need to change about ourselves. It is accepting that our contentment comes from within, in the here and now, exactly as things are. It is accepting that we can't find lasting happiness outside of ourselves, and that happiness isn't a destination over there, it's in the here and now. It is accepting each and every moment and sitting with the uncomfortable concept of accepting life just as it is. The list we could make would go on and on for eternity, because it is acceptance of everything just as it is and was and will be.

Acceptance doesn't mean we don't try. On the contrary, it means we engage more fully as the outcomes available to us are truly limitless, limited only by what we think we can accomplish. With this knowledge, when doors shut in our face, we keep trying and thinking differently. It is not about wishing the past went a different way. It's accepting it. It's not about saying, "I wish I would have said or done 'that'. If only 'x' or 'y' would have happened, then I'd be fine/happy/content." It is looking at current state in life with total acceptance, knowing I did my best at the time and I am doing the best that I can today.

It doesn't mean I don't want to change my current path in this present moment. It doesn't mean I don't have struggles. It doesn't negate that I was clearly wronged by someone or that what they did to me was horrible. It means that I accept current state exactly as it is, because it is a fact and I cannot change that. This can be frustrating when our ego is screaming, "But we are/were right, and they are/were wrong." That may be true, but when we sit with acceptance, we accept all that is; good and bad, right and wrong.

Sitting in acceptance doesn't mean we sit idly by and give up. We are change agents and can absolutely (and must) use this present moment to shape our today and our future. When we bring intention into the equation, we know that the actions and choices we make today influence the present moment and the future. What we do today does matter, to some extent. I say to some extent, because regardless of our choices today, certain variables are out there in the world that are outside of our immediate control, but we keep trying and performing intentional actions.

When we sit with acceptance, we come to the sometimes harsh realization that in present moment, we are the sum total of our choices up to this point. And I know that's a loaded statement, but it's true. I am the sum total of my choices up to this point in my life. I hated that expression when I first heard it. "What do you mean I am the sum total of my choices?" My ego wants to tell me that I am the victim of circumstance. I am the martyr. "Look what I put up with! You think I chose this? I would quit if I could, but I can't because (insert fear statement)." Or, "Look how they treat me though; you think I want that? Once 'x' happens, I'll finally be happy. I just need 'x' to happen and everything will be fine!" Sadly, that is not the case. Some other form of unhappiness will take over, and this is why we need to find acceptance, and find our true contentment and fulfillment from within, in present moment, instead of trying to find it outside of ourselves based on our job title, our salary, our possessions or how we look on the outside.

Very few people in life do not have a choice when it comes to changing their lives. The other options may not be comfortable or easy, but 99.9% of the time, there is an alternative choice. Staying is a choice, and there's nothing wrong with that choice. Just bring your awareness to this. Sometimes that's the only choice we feel like we have or can see for today, and that is ok. Accept that as uncomfortable as that may be.

Think of a situation where you see no choice. Now take a step back and try to come at the situation from someone else's perspective so it's not as personal for you. Write out all the possible choices, and see if in fact there are other choices available. There will be. And when we know this, we are awakened to the infinite possibilities in front of us. This may feel overwhelming at first, but try to see how empowering it can be. We bring awareness to the endless choices that are still available for us to make. Instead of fear and regret, we sit with acceptance of where we are today, knowing it was our choices that got us here, and it is our choices that will keep us where we are or our choices that will change our today and shape our future.

I said this was hard for me the first time I heard it, because I always thought life happened and I was just along for the ride. I didn't think I had many choices in my life. In reality, I always had choices. I had thousands of choices each day, but when I associated with the ego, it told me I was the victim or martyr. "Poor me," is one of the ego's favorite games to play. I didn't consciously choose to be the victim or martyr in my stories, but I was definitely playing the part. I was so heavily associated as one with my thoughts. I was unaware that I could be separate from my thoughts, and therefore, I believed the egoic voice in my head when it told me how I had been wronged. My ego told me how entitled I was to something better. That if this person or that situation wasn't holding me back, I'd be fine. It's their fault or circumstance's fault. When in actuality, I chose to stay in 'x' situation, be it a friendship, relationship, job/work environment or other. It was my choice. It is always my choice. I always had a choice, but I didn't always know this.

The alternative choice may be overwhelming, but it is a choice to stay or quit. I was at a job for many years that I was good at. It paid well and it had great benefits. The only problem was that it made me miserable. I dreaded going to work and only loved the weekends and vacations and pay day. After many years, one day I came to the realization that I was choosing to stay. It was my choice not to leave. I was choosing to stay in an environment that was not conducive to what I wanted to do. I was so numb for so long that I didn't realize this. I didn't wake up one day and quit, because I had rent and bills to pay. But once I realized it was a choice, I realized I could make other choices. I updated my resume, I took several certificate courses online that were of interest to me, and I applied to over 40 jobs. Two companies interviewed me and I didn't get either job. It was wonderful! Why? Because it gave me hope! I was able to see all the choices I now had. Taking the online trainings helped me see the passion I had and helped me to ultimately leave that job.

The last year I was at that job was such a different experience for me because I had changed. I was no longer a victim, but an empowered individual who was choosing to stay for the time being as I worked on next steps for my career. Because of that awareness, the energy I gave changed. I saw the work environment I was in for what it was and I no longer personalized it. Many flourished in that fast-paced environment, but I did not. It took all my energy because I inadvertently gave it my energy. Once I realized my energy is for me and I'm not going to give it away so freely, I no longer gave it to my job, and I left on a high note. I made the choice to stay, worked on myself, and ultimately made the choice to leave months later, without anger and resentment.

This couldn't have happened if I had not come to accept everything as it was, and also accept the fact of the role I played in it all of it. Once I realized I had a choice, my hope returned and I was better able to act in accordance with what I wanted for tomorrow, while living in present moment. I started living for myself, respecting others, but putting myself in a position that supported me, and brought me inner contentment and fulfillment. The job wasn't as painful once I realized I was choosing to stay. It was more pleasurable and I enjoyed it more. Nothing else had changed except my perspective, and this awareness was liberating.

With acceptance, we can begin to find the neutrality of any situation. There is no storytelling. It simply is or it simply was. Did it happen to me or did it merely happen? We take the drama out of the situation and sit with acceptance. When we are storytelling, we are often telling ourselves our own version of the story and denying acceptance of what is and what was, paying attention only to the details that favor our version of the story we are telling ourselves or others. Acceptance takes the highs and lows out of the drama we create and the stories we tell ourselves, creating a separation from the egoic thoughts.

This brings us back to living peacefully in present moment. It doesn't mean what happened to us wasn't wrong. It may have been. And it doesn't mean we don't try to improve a situation. Knowing we have choices, we can change and improve a situation, if only realizing we are choosing to stay, and we do that with a knowing—an intention.

With acceptance, I accept that I am human. I accept that humans are fallible, and therefore as a human, I too will make mistakes. I accept that I will always have thoughts, as that is also part of being human. We have thoughts up until our last breath, and telling myself to not have thoughts is futile. Believe me, I've tried for over 40 years. I accept that I cannot stop thought, but I can change how I interact with my thoughts or redirect my thinking, working to change negative patterned thinking. I accept that with my fallibility of being a human, I am still amazing. I am *PERFECTLY* Imperfect in every way!

The flip side of this is trying to accept what goes on in our world daily. It is overwhelmingly tragic. People are murdered and tortured, and wars rage on. Many people are treated unfairly, and education and healthcare have become a luxury many cannot afford. Much of this is done at the hands of others who are so attached to their egos and their beliefs that they see nothing harmful in what they are doing. This is tragically sad. And the worst part is that I can't change any of it in the immediate present moment. I sit with it, accept it, and I look to myself and ask, "What can I do today to make a difference?"

If I am to sit in acceptance of these atrocities, one could say that means I am being passive and allowing it. And I fully disagree. When I sit in acceptance, I can still say that what is happening is horrible and tragic, and, I can act today to make changes for the future, while in present moment. I cannot change what happened, but I can use my voice to help people understand how attached to their egos they are to start changing the system from the inside out. It doesn't mean I agree with it or support it or like it, but I have to accept what is happening because it is what it is. This is the turning point for us. With this awareness, we can launch into action in present moment in hopes of making a better today and tomorrow.

One such action was creating ImperfectionWellness.com and Possley's Paradigm, two free resources to help people get unstuck from association with their thoughts and patterned behaviors. When I left my job, I felt called to share this paradigm freely around the world with children and adults alike. I want it to be easily accessible to anyone and everyone. I want our elected officials to see this paradigm. I want children to learn it in school. I want employers to offer trainings on it to their employees. This idea doesn't negate the wars and hatred that are occurring daily, but it starts planting a seed that there are other options; that all of us can make other choices. It's a painfully slow process, but it has to start somewhere. If not now, when?

I accept that the system as it's currently set up allows for the atrocities of present moment throughout the world. I have to, they are occurring right in front of me. But it doesn't mean I am complacent or approve of them. Acceptance is not approval. It is looking at current state and then shifting my actions based on what I can do to work towards a better tomorrow. It's uncomfortable to say the least. It's a modern tragedy that people so stuck in egoic thinking don't know any other way other than oppressing others, because they believe it when their ego says, "There isn't enough to go around, so we must oppress others."

I made some tough choices to leave my corporate NYC life behind because I knew there was more I could do, more I needed to do. My hope is that this awareness opens people's eyes so we are no longer sleepwalking through life. I hope it inspires people and resonates with them. I know that I can't solve for world peace today, but I can start by affecting one person at a time, starting with myself, then by teaching others. I can bring awareness of attachment to ego into the consciousness of our world, in hopes of making a better tomorrow as many before me already have. This universal truth is out there, we just don't know about it and need to get it into the collective consciousness of all.

Sitting with acceptance can be quite challenging. The easier option is to repress or suppress the feelings we have and create a story out of it to tell ourselves and our friends. We distract, escape, numb and avoid. We shop, drink, eat, do drugs; anything to numb and help us deal with our current reality. In the moment, it seems easy to ignore it, to push it down, to "just get over it". But when we do that, we create additional layers of stress on ourselves. We are now storing the stress which comes out later, usually stronger and more violent than when it went in. As the arsenal grows over the years, we have this reserve of anger and negativity to pull from and carrying this around year after year becomes exhausting. This is why we sit in acceptance, center ourselves, set an intention, and perform next right action in the present moment. This is my wish for you. This is my wish for all of us.

Sitting in the Discomfort of Acceptance:

I accept things as they are right now in this moment, accepting the "is-ness" of life and the world as it is, was and will be.

I am aware that acceptance doesn't mean that we sit idly by. This awareness empowers us to set an intention and perform next right action (see Chapter 13) instead of mindlessly going through life feeling like we don't have a say in what happens.

I accept that most of what happens in this world is outside of my direct control, but I do have a voice and I do have influence and can always set an intention and perform next right action.

Sitting in acceptance centers me and brings me back to present moment; empowering me for the choices I make today that will shape my future.

I accept where I am in this very moment of my life, knowing I am the sum total of all of my choices up to this point in my life. I may not like the choice(s) I have made or the current choices I have, but I know that I always have a choice, and doing nothing is a choice.

I sit in full acceptance of my body, my hair, my skin color, my voice, my height, my weight, my age, and any other characteristic I identify with as I let go of the ego's need to judge, rate and compare myself to others.

I accept everything about me right here and right now, whether I can change it or not. This may feel uncomfortable, but keep coming back to unconditional love and full acceptance of self!

I accept that I was hurt by you, or that I hurt you and I am moving on, apologizing if necessary and forgiving you/forgiving self if necessary. This may mean unfriending someone, and/or setting clear boundaries for a relationship, as I am now aware that I have choices in my interactions with others.

When I am fighting acceptance, stress arises and I may start pulling in thoughts and prior experiences (storytelling) and start living in the past or future with these thoughts (time traveling). I remind myself that acceptance does not equal approval of what is happening or what has happened.

Sitting in acceptance helps me come back to the beauty of present moment, as uncomfortable as it may feel. I know the only place I will find lasting contentment and fulfillment is from within in this present moment. We remove ourselves from the argument of what "should" be versus what is or what was or what will be. It is all meaningless speculation. We learn to accept and embrace the present moment "is-ness" of life in all its forms then set an intention and perform next right action.

8

Be the Observer

I create space in my consciousness by becoming the observer of my thoughts. They come from me, but when I observe them, I realize I am more than my thoughts!

W e now know that we have thoughts and always will, and we are aware that this is outside of our control, as it is a part of being human. We know that we are separate from our thoughts, yet we are still having them. What are we to do when we have strong emotional thoughts? What do we do when we associate or identify with them?

Another technique I learned many years ago is to become the observer of our thoughts. As we have let go of the idea that we can control having thoughts, now we choose to observe them, knowing they will always keep coming. When we become the observer, we realize that our thoughts, feelings and emotions are impermanent, that they come and go as they please. This awareness removes the power our thoughts have over us. It neutralizes our thoughts so much that many times they become entertaining because we no longer let ourselves be defined by them.

Many of our thoughts circle in our brains as ruminating thoughts. I once heard that out of the thousands of thoughts we have each and every day, over 90% of those thoughts are the same ones as the day before (and likely the day before that). If all of these thoughts are the same ones as the day(s) prior, then we know we are not living in the present moment, but reliving and fearing the past and future respectively.

For me, the stories my ego tells me are rarely on par with what happened in the past or what we will happen in the future. They are stories, fragments, and half-truths that take me on a wild roller coaster ride if I choose to associate with them and believe them. When we become the observer, we can choose to get off the roller coaster ride of being powerless against our ego-driven thoughts and start watching the ride instead of helplessly being on it. We step into present moment where life is happening and unfolding in front of us. We are now able to make choices that align with True Self instead of being frozen in the past or future in storytelling mode. When we become the observer, we become liberated from our egoic thoughts. Some of the thoughts I have are based in experience; the things I think about did happen. When we loosen our attachment with our thoughts and become the observer, it doesn't mean we negate our experiences. It means that we are lessening the emotional hold the thoughts and experiences have over us.

I was diagnosed with metastatic testicular cancer at 18. It was a very emotional time for me going through two major surgeries and several months of chemotherapy. When I associate as one with my egoic thoughts, I am a victim who almost died of cancer. When I am the observer and loosen my attachment, I was a young man who was diagnosed with cancer, survived, and went on to live and continue to live a fulfilling life. I become empowered. There were struggles during that time, but I am not at one with the struggle. I had the struggle, but the emotional connection is lost. I still have the memory of going through my treatments, but I am now more than that memory and the ego's commentary about that time in my life. This experience has given me strength in my life. I am a proud survivor, not a victim and not stuck in 1992, the year I was diagnosed.

To be the observer means we observe our thoughts as they are. We don't judge them, rate them or try to change them. If we begin to judge or rate or try to change them, that is the ego coming back in, creating an endless cycle of reidentification with thought. Initially, the thoughts may be uncomfortable to observe. Over time, as we realize we are the observer, we become separate from the thoughts (or feelings and emotions) and over time they lose their power over us. We observe the many thoughts as they come and go, bringing back awareness that we will always have them and always will. We are aware that they are random and are only a partial truth or partial version of what actually happened or may happen. We are aware that these thoughts take us out of present moment and back into storytelling. We no longer need to suppress, repress, escape or numb ourselves to avoid having our thoughts, feelings and emotions. We experience them, feel them, observe them, knowing they too shall pass. We have them, but we are not them. They do not define who we are.

To make the concept of being the observer easier for me, I would mentally sit in a folding lawn chair on the side of the road and picture my thoughts going by as a parade. It helped me detach from the thoughts and put distance between them and me. You could also picture your thoughts as clouds going by in the sky, or as a movie being projected onto a large movie screen. You watch the clouds and the movie, holding onto the awareness of being separate from the thoughts, what they are, and what they say about you. They are harmless and are never-ending. They will always be there, and when you are the observer, you separate from associating as one with the thoughts. You separate from being held hostage by your thoughts or by being a victim or martyr of your thoughts. You are simply the observer. This helps us come back to living in the present moment, away from our thoughts and the untrue stories they tell us about ourselves and others. When doing this, the thoughts may even become entertaining (*let's see what story the ego has created*) as opposed to feeling or having attachment or identification that *these thoughts are me*. It becomes, "While I have those thoughts, I am separate from them, and they do not define me." More space is created in our consciousness, which allows us to break free from identification as one with our thoughts, feelings and emotions.

Becoming the observer was a challenge for me in the beginning. I often pictured myself in the eye of the storm with thoughts, feelings, emotions and stories swirling around me. I sat above looking down on this and was the observer of it all as everything swirled around me, feeling safe in the eye of the storm. At times, I would try to rate or change my thoughts, or I ended up reidentifying with the thoughts and the story. I would fight it and wanted to flee or avoid it all together. But over time, I came back to being the observer. Observing myself sitting in the eye of the storm helped prevent me from reidentifying them, and over time I even smiled and laughed as my ego mind tried to hook me back into an emotional response to the thoughts. Sometimes I'd be hooked, and as soon as I realized I was, I became aware and returned to being the observer.

When I am associated as one with my thoughts, I begin to have feelings about the thoughts. These emotions I am feeling are real, but we begin to break apart our association with them as we observe them. Additionally, when we say, "I am angry" or "I am sad and depressed," this creates an association link of belief that we are the emotion instead of being the person who is having the emotion. An easy way to change this is to reframe what we say. For example, try saying, "I feel angry," instead of saying "I am an angry person." This allows us to have the fleeting feeling as opposed to being identified as one with or defined by the feeling or emotion.

The same holds true for how we identify with our thoughts. I've changed from, "I am my thoughts and what they say about me," to "I am with thought and I am having thoughts. I am separate from my thoughts and what they say about me and the world around me." I also know my thoughts are fleeting and transient. Many times, these thoughts can be negative. "If my thoughts say I am stupid and worthless, I guess I am stupid and worthless." This is not the case, but when we are identified as one with the thought, we may feel stupid and worthless. We change this to, "I am having a thought that says I am stupid and worthless. I am going to observe this because I know I am separate from this thought. It is false and fleeting, and the thought will likely return, so I will continue to watch it because it is simply not true."

Each time we become the observer, we create some separation, some space from these intrusive and pervasive thoughts. We have moments of clarity that may start off lasting only a few seconds. Once we build this skill over time, the clarity we have will last for days on end where we remain separate from the thoughts and what they say about us. We always remind ourselves we are not fighting the thoughts. That would be futile as they are always there. We remind ourselves that we will observe them. Sometimes, I will smile or break into laughter when the thoughts arise because I know what is going on now, and I realize how absurd some of the thoughts are.

> When I become the observer of my thoughts, I discover that who
> I am is not what I think.

Additionally, the ego is not always mean. Sometimes it tells me I am amazing and better than others. "Nothing can get me now. I'm invincible," is what the egoic thought will say. I am just as aware when this happens. I have come to realize that when I am thinking about my thinking, or holding myself above or below someone else, then I am likely associated with an egoic thought pattern and not living as True Self. Regardless, if it tells me I walk on water or if I'm worthless, I now know that neither are True Self.

If I need someone to give me a compliment, or I want to be validated by a job or title or material item to give me my self-worth, then I know I am in egoic thinking. I become aware, and I bring compassion and non-judgment back into the picture as the observer. I refrain from comparisons and I merely observe the thought, good or bad, coming back to present moment. Do I enjoy the job or title or material items still? Perhaps. But now I am not identified with it. My identity doesn't change because these external things and titles and accolades do not define me.

This is a tough step because many people are strongly associated with their thoughts and feel like "I am my thoughts." I am here to say that you are separate from your thoughts. As I've said several times already, "I am more than what my thoughts say about me and the world around me!" I have been working on this for over 10 years, and there are still times when I get fooled into believing I am my thoughts. It's so subtle. It's like I took the bait and was hooked and before I realized it, my mood was affected because I had associated yet again with my negative thoughts. But each time, I realize sooner that I did before that I have associated with my thoughts, and I become the observer much faster. Take time with this and have self-compassion, knowing you will get hooked by your thoughts time and time again, but this will pass. You are now aware of how to be the observer.

Practicing How to Be the Observer:

I become the observer, the witness of my thoughts and that voice from within, aware that I am separate from it: "Hello ego/egoic thoughts, I see you and I am currently feeling the effects of you, but I also know I am separate from you. I am separate from the stories you tell me and I am going to observe you without judgment and be in this present moment. I am the observer."

As the observer, I am aware it is impossible to stop my thoughts. I am alive; therefore, I have thoughts. I choose to be separate from my thoughts by observing them, as I sit in the eye of the storm and I watch them as they circle around me, as a parade going by, or as the watcher of a movie. Instead of being in the parade or movie, I pull back and observe the thoughts and memories as they go by, knowing I have them but I am separate from them, and it's in this space where I am liberated from identification with my thoughts.

As I observe my thoughts, I can also say, "Next," if I am stuck on an unpleasant thought that won't go away. Mentally *swipe left* and move on, knowing the thought isn't the real you.

I don't rate the thoughts as good or bad; right or wrong. I observe and sometimes smile at the antics my egoic thoughts have, as they are usually false, inflated or deflated from the actual situation or stories my ego is telling me based on fragments and half-truths of what really happened.

When I rate or judge the thoughts or try to stop them, I have reassociated with my ego and am now in a tug-of-war with trying to change or stop my thoughts. This is a futile effort, so I remind myself to let go of judgment, stop trying to change them and return to being the observer.

9

Surrender

When I am overwhelmed and feeling out of control, I surrender to God, the Divine, Energy, Source, Spirit, Nature or the Universe—a higher power that is outside of me, and greater than me.

S urrender is an active process whereby we relinquish control and attach-ment to the things, people, our problems and the world around us. We enjoy living in this world, realizing we can be in it and not of it, knowing we are defined by more than what we think and what we have. Surrender involves trusting something outside of us; something greater than us. Many people surrender to God, a higher power, energy, source, spirit, nature or the universe. We are surrendering to what is, the present moment, to what was, the past, and to what will be, the future. This is in alignment with the concept of acceptance of what is, was and will be.

Surrender is letting go of the idea of control; letting go of the belief that "I can control everything in my environment." We also surrender any resistance we may have so we can accept what is, was or will be. Surrender can be thought of as "dropping the oars" of the rowboat, even getting out of the boat and being the water instead of constantly rowing upstream. It is also becoming aware of the idea that while I have influence over my future, I also know there are many things in the future out of my direct control, and I am ok with that as I surrender.

Surrender is finding peace with the natural flow of what life has to offer. When we surrender, it is easier to sit in acceptance. This doesn't mean our actions don't influence or shape tomorrow. It simply means we know things may work out differently than we had planned. We can still work towards a goal, knowing the outcome may take more time or be different than what we originally planned. We are aware of the many variables outside of our control and we become ok with this, knowing everything will work out for the best.

When we surrender, we relinquish the idea that we can control each of life's variables. Surrendering does not mean that we don't try. It does not mean we give up. It does not mean we become passive in life or that we don't care. It means we are actively engaged in living life and making choices, but there are forces beyond us, outside of our control, and we are along for the ride, while we make engaging choices for today and tomorrow. Thing may turn out differently than we planned and by surrendering, we learn to be ok with this.

We also surrender in an attempt to transcend our intellect and the ego. While the intellect is helpful when it comes to supporting us with logic and reasoning, this is counterintuitive from the perspective of surrender as we are discussing it here. When we surrender, we are going beyond the limitations of the intellect and ego. We are going beyond what the intellect's logic and the ego's thoughts say. We are going beyond the need we have to control, analyze and predict as well as going beyond the endless commentary provided by the ego.

Yes, we can apply intellect and strategy and reasoning in life when necessary, like with intentional thinking of an architect building a bridge or a medical provider diagnosing a complex case or a student learning complex physics, but we can also transcend this and come back to present moment. This frees us to sit in acceptance of life as it unfolds, knowing we don't need to "figure it all out." Instead, we can sit in the awe of what is, set an intention and perform next right action from this centered place, allowing for a deeper connection with life.

Many times, when I am struggling and attached to what I want or how I want a situation to go, I am so engrossed with my thoughts and what "must happen my way", that I can't find a solution, or I freak out when something doesn't go as planned. The stress and anxiety grow, and suddenly I am in full alert panic mode. It is at this moment when I choose to take a step back, and I choose to walk away from the problem. I literally hold my hands out and say, "This is bigger than me. I am letting go and you (God, source, etc.) are going to take care of this for me." After an hour, a good night's sleep, or maybe even a few days later, I suddenly have the answer, other options, or there is a simple solution. My panic mind couldn't see the answer right in front of me. Only by surrendering do these answers clearly appear.

I am a former control freak and I had a career in healthcare regulatory compliance. I was the rule follower. The rules were comfortable. The rules forced "control" over a situation. This crept into my personal life, and everything became black and white. Creating gray, embracing gray and living in gray became such an amazing thing once I let go of control and fully surrendered. Now I feel so much more at ease. I still make decisions, I still plan and strategize and act accordingly, but now I am able to follow the flow of life, knowing all will be ok. I surrender knowing I still make decisions and live my life, but I know there are many variables beyond my control and I am ok with this.

By surrendering we are able to learn and grow through mistakes and experiences, while easily adapting to new circumstances. We build resiliency and vulnerability, bringing us closer to those we care about. We are able to better enjoy the flow of life, leaning more into our intuition, releasing the need to control everything. When we surrender, we learn that we don't have to carry the weight of the world on our shoulders. It's liberating that God, the Divine or other can take the reins as we drop the oars, get out of the boat and become the water, letting the current flow where it flows.

One day when I was coming back from a stressful week-long trip, I went to check in for my flight, only to find out it was canceled. Without realizing it, my ego was activated and I was infuriated. They booked me on a red-eye, getting in a 6am the next day. I tried to get onto other flights for the day and everything was booked. I became aware that my ego was activated, so I took a few deep breaths while sitting in acceptance of what was happening. Once I calmed down and was no longer associated with my entitled ego that insisted I get onto the next direct flight home, and I slowly started to surrender. I could feel myself starting to relax and decided to call the airline instead of trying to rebook on their website. I talked to an agent who put me on a direct flight the next day. She also told me the airline would likely reimburse me for my hotel stay since they had canceled last minute and couldn't get me on a flight that day.

I went to the hotel and relaxed by the pool for the afternoon before coming back to my room and falling asleep. I awoke the next day, got on my flight and made it home without incident. I submitted my hotel receipt, and sure enough, I was reimbursed for my hotel stay. The old me would have handled the situation very differently, and I likely would have had a stress headache from fighting that present moment reality of the canceled flight.

By utilizing the concepts of awareness, acceptance and surrender, I was able to enjoy an unexpected extra day by the pool, relaxing and meditating. When I surrendered that day, I even said to myself, my preference is to get home today, but unless I pay for a new flight, that isn't going to happen, and I don't have a conflict tomorrow, so what's the harm. This was my personal proof of concept of the paradigm in action. It was working through me as my roadmap to coming back to present moment as True Self. It was such an amazing experience and I learned so much about how I've grown over time. This is why we practice the paradigm when things are calm so we can respond accordingly when things are out of our control, like with a flat tire, a canceled flight or a myriad of other situations where we can begin to surrender.

When I surrender, I work to find acceptance in all situations without struggle, remembering the adage that *insistence equals resistance*. When I surrender, I am working to find my inner courage. I become emotionally stronger. Surrendering doesn't mean you like an outcome, nor does it mean you don't have negative feelings and emotions around an outcome. It means you know it is out of your control and you find acceptance over time.

Surrender is not giving up. Surrender helps break our attachments to outcomes and helps us overcome resistance to becoming our True Selves, while making us more resilient. When we surrender, we can move from fighting a situation to embracing a situation, knowing we may need time, but we know this too shall pass. Surrendering allows us to be more vulnerable, which allows us to build stronger relationships to those around us. We surrender to any idea of perfection, knowing it doesn't exist. Knowing all of this, I surrender.

Surrendering:

I surrender to God, the Divine, Energy, Source, Spirit, Nature or the Universe—a higher power that is outside of me, and greater than me.

When I surrender, I relinquish control of what is outside of my direct control. I surrender the idea that I can control the entire world around me, while at the same time, I am aware that I can influence the world around me based on my actions.

When I can't see a way out, when I am lost or when I am overwhelmed, I surrender knowing I am more than these thoughts and these situations. When it is more than I can handle, I know through surrender, doors will open and solutions will appear. I surrender to what is too much for me to handle at this moment, knowing it will all be answered in time.

I know through surrender I can let someone or something else handle the big decisions when I don't feel like I can make one or when things aren't working out as I planned.

When I surrender, I become stronger because I am now open to asking for and receiving help in all its various forms, repeating to myself, "I am open, I allow, I surrender."

I surrender to any resistance I may be feeling, and resistance is a normal part of the process. When I find myself in resistance, I have self-compassion and remove any judgment. I fully surrender myself to unconditional self-love.

I surrender to only feeling comfortable. I know all that is comfortable is not good, and all that is good is not comfortable. I continue to surrender and breath through any discomfort with self-compassion.

I surrender to transcend my intellect in order to center myself and embrace life as it unfolds for me in the present moment.

I surrender because I care, knowing that when I surrender, it will work itself out.

10

Lean In & Let Go

Letting go is turning inward, and leaning into the discomfort, releasing stored feelings and emotions. In letting go, I gain the freedom to no longer carry stored emotional burdens.

M any of us carry emotional connections to past events. While we had the past experience and can often recall it, letting go of the emotional attachment we have to it can be liberating. By letting go, we don't negate that we had the experience or try to forget it. Instead, we acknowledge the experience and lessen our emotional response and our connection to it. We can let go of a certain belief about ourselves or someone else. We can let go of the emotional pain we have connected to an experience. We can let go of the stress, worry, anxiety and sadness of what has happened to us and what is going on around us. We do this not so that we live in a bubble, but so that we can break free from the chains of self-oppression and live more fully, while being more present in our lives for ourselves and those around us.

So often, unprocessed experiences get stored in our bodies. Something happens to us and we either suppress it (consciously) or repress it (unconsciously). For example, the bullying I endured growing up, that many others have also experienced, wasn't processed for many years and was stored in my body, whether I realized it or not, and came out in other ways that affected my day to day living. Or, we may have had a parent or loved one say something in the moment, like, "You're too much, you always mess up" and we then carry that memory with us consciously or unconsciously for years. This can manifest in our lives as uncontrolled anger or a limiting, patterned behavior or false self-belief about ourselves.

We may have been made fun of in a social situation as a child and may not realize how this affects us, and then our egoic voice tells us an exaggerated version of the story, and we are now convinced that we have social anxiety, instead of the likely reality that we may feel anxious in social situations. This is a distinction to differentiate how we speak to ourselves. To lean in and let go is to sit with one of these stories we tell ourselves, or to sit with a thought, a feeling or emotion, and let it come to the surface instead of pushing it back down or numbing to avoid the feeling. We feel the emotional energy and let it be as it passes through us so it is no longer being stored inside of us. When you do this and as you feel the discomfort, you lean into it and breath through it, no longer suppressing or repressing it. You release the stored energy behind that memory and let it dissipate instead of continuing to store it where it can haunt us for years.

Leaning in and letting go is sitting with and breathing through the fear and ugly feelings. It is sitting with the feelings and emotions while we lean into the discomfort, allowing it to come to the surface, as we continue breathing through it. Instead of trying to consciously suppress it, instead of trying to escape it through other distractions or numb it through other behaviors, we fully feel it as it is. We sit with it as the observer. We don't try to outrun it or ignore it. We do not rate it or compare it or judge it. We simply sit in the discomfort and breath through it for several minutes until the sensation passes.

The thoughts that "hooked me" were usually on the negative side of the spectrum and were internalized from some past experience in my life. The voice within said anything from, "You are overwhelming and too much," to, "You are fat, ugly, and worthless." This hurt me so much because it was coming from me, from my thoughts, from experiences I was having in the world around me, and I believed it. It was so painful that I repressed it for years based on experiences from over 40 years ago that were haunting daily without any awareness of this on my part.

Your experiences may be different, but regardless, these thought patterns and self-beliefs that all of us have create our narrative and influence our feelings and emotions and how we feel about ourselves and the world around us. We are likely not aware of this because it's been repressed for so long. We are not aware of how these repressed experiences affect us in our daily lives. We have skewed self-beliefs about ourselves based on these experiences and thought patterns we are unknowingly identified with. When we become aware of this, we can begin to let go by letting these feelings and beliefs come to the surface so we can address them and let go of the pain and false self-beliefs that tell us we're less than or better than someone. We let go of the stories, the self-beliefs and the scars left behind from these past experiences.

This is why awareness is such an important step for me. I often fall into unconscious living, going through motions, without awareness of the present moment. One day I had a feeling that something was off. I didn't know what it was, and I wasn't able to put it into words. I felt a mental block. I wanted to address it, but I didn't know how to since I wasn't aware of the underlying emotion behind what I was feeling. As hard as it was, I sat in the moment and continued to feel this awkward feeling, being aware of my present surroundings, breathing through the discomfort, reassuring myself I was safe and ok, as I applied the technique of leaning in and letting go. Within a matter of minutes, the feeling subsided and I felt an emotional release. I was no longer storing or carrying the emotional burden.

If you can't identify an emotion, see if you have a feeling that predominates. Is that feeling tied to an event? To a thought? To a person? Start wherever you are, being aware of a thought, feeling or emotion, and lean into that as a starting place. Bring this awareness to how you feel. When I first started to lean in and let go, I wasn't aware of how my thoughts affected my emotions, thereby affecting how I felt. Now that I am aware of this, the process is much easier for me.

You may be asking yourself, "Why would I want to sit through something painful like this? Why would I want to lean in & let go if I can just avoid it and push it down?" Because as my best friend Kendall always said to me in times of stress, fear and anxiety, "The only way out is through." Meaning, we address this head on instead of going around it or distracting ourselves from addressing it. We work through it instead of storing it or numbing ourselves and trying to escape it. These tactics are temporary fixes that can ultimately lead to depression, anxiety, fear and anger to name a few. Instead of avoiding or masking by overindulging in drinking, smoking, exercising, shopping or emotional eating, etc., we face it, breathe through it, and let it pass. We still have the memories, but we don't carry the emotional baggage anymore because we've let go of the trapped emotional energy stored in our body.

With the lean in & let go process, we sit with the discomfort and realize it is a passing thought, feeling or emotion, and we are releasing it in a safe space, on our terms. It can no longer haunt us. Usually, we have these stress moments magnified in our head as a false reality or an exaggeration of what happened. We have told ourselves the story for so long, we now just assume it is a part of us. That it is a part of our character and who we are and we are at one with it. Many times, it is based in a past reality, clouded by stories and half-truths we have told ourselves about it. Or it is based in a story fragment that we've made so much bigger than what it actually was.

In learning to sit with our feelings and emotion, we learn to refrain from any judgment about them, learning to release them instead of storing them inside of us and holding onto them as part of our identity. We relinquish the idea that these battle wounds are a part of us that we must carry with us for life. While the situation or experience that is causing the emotion did happen to us, we learn that we can let go of the emotional response we have to it, while still knowing it happened. It doesn't take that experience away from you. Letting go doesn't mean what happened was right or wrong for that matter. Instead, it lets you have the experience you had, while relinquishing the emotional toll it has had over you. The process is deceptively simple. It's deceptively simple in that we may not appreciate how such a simple process like leaning into our suppressed and repressed experiences, allowing ourselves to feel our emotions without judgement, and letting go of the trapped energy can release mountains of age-old emotions and their effects on us in such a simple manner. But it does.

> When we lean in and let go, we begin to release the emotional attachment we have with an experience. We will likely always remember it, but we are letting go of the emotional hold it has over us which prevents us from fully enjoying the present moment. The energy it used to take to suppress and repress the feelings can now be used to release the energy and heal so we can live more authentically.

We are learning to move on from our fears, feelings and emotions, about these past experiences, not by numbing, escaping and distracting ourselves, but by addressing them head on. We are no longer the story we tell ourselves about ourselves (going back to the example of do I have social anxiety (story) vs. I feel anxious in social situations). If I am aware of the latter and feel anxious sometimes, I now know that the feelings are real but don't tell the whole story, and I can push through that next social situation without using numbing agents (e.g. drugs and alcohol) and/or I can stop avoiding situations and deal with these feelings head on. Lean into where this story originally started and work from there as you let go of the story you are telling yourself that's now holding you back.

In life, we sometimes choose, though often inadvertently, to continue to avoid dealing with these feelings by distraction and escapism, because we seek comfort. And as I said in the surrender exercise, all that is comfortable is not good, and all that is good is not comfortable. Initially, the idea of sitting with my thoughts and examining them was too much for me and did not feel comfortable at all, but over time the benefit of releasing the energy outweighed the discomfort. The idea of leaning in & letting go was overwhelming and I wanted to avoid sitting with these feelings. It's part of the reason why I drank so much. When I drank, the feelings and emotions were kept at bay. But this was a band-aid. By avoiding dealing with these past experiences and holding onto them for dear life, we pay a price of physical and psychological illnesses. Releasing this emotional baggage far outweighs a few moments of discomfort when we lean it and let go. Sitting with this less comfortable feeling is fleeting, as is the emotional response once it's released. It too shall pass, once we center ourselves, lean in, breathe through the discomfort and begin to let go of these past emotional experiences.

Learning how to lean in and let go was instrumental for me. I was able to sit with my thoughts and feelings, tie them in with an emotion, and let go of my association as being associated or identified as one with them. It gave me back my power of living as True Self. I needed to move past these mental blocks. I was ready to feel the fear, go to the places that scared me, and let go. It was time to break free from the shackles that held me back for so long.

In all honesty, the first time I tried this technique, it was a challenge for me. I felt the emotion and physically leaned in. I had to lean in because all I wanted to do was run, to distract myself, to numb myself. But I wasn't going to run this time. My chest was tight and I was overwhelmed. I felt the pain of the emotion coming up, and I didn't want to face it. The emotion coming out felt like it did going in; it felt horribly uncomfortable and terrible. But I knew keeping it suppressed wouldn't help me either, so this time I chose to let it out and release it.

I got up from the couch and took some deep breaths, almost stopping, but I sat back down. Again, I leaned in, and as I breathed in and out, I mentally surrendered to the emotion and felt it. I felt the discomfort, I felt the shame, embarrassment and self-loathing. I felt the painful emotions I had around being told, "You are too much." I felt that pain and I continued to breathe. I kept saying to myself, "let it go, let it go" as I continued with intentional slow, deep breaths. I refrained from any judgment. I labeled it as it was, a painful past experience I had and I was letting the emotional energy behind it pass.

I felt the feeling fully and let it come bubbling up so it could dissipate into nothingness. Once that happened, it could no longer harm me. I didn't judge the feeling or thoughts associated with it. I continued being the observer, surrendering and letting go. I said to myself, "I am more than this and I will continue breathing through this pain and this feeling." I just let it be as it was with the awareness of however it felt going in is how it will feel coming out, a key point to remember.

In what felt like forever, but in all reality, was only a few minutes, I realized I had truly let go. I let go of my attachment with the feeling and sat there leaning in, not avoiding or distracting or ignoring. And just like that, suddenly out of nowhere, the heavy emotional feeling magically melted away. It just dissipated. It suddenly disappeared and my tight chest relaxed. It felt like the largest emotional weight was lifted off of me. I actually felt the benefits of this technique in the moment! It was just amazing. As tough as the process was for me to sit through the first time, it became much easier over time. Now, when I am out of alignment and have a gnawing uncomfortable feeling, I actively engage in this process to fully feel the feeling or emotion, knowing the emotional response lessen over time.

I also realized some emotional responses will likely come up more than once. I say this so you are aware that it is not always a one and done situation when you lean in and let go and everything is fine. You may have to repeat the process, but each additional time it comes up, more is released and the emotional response continues to lessen. I had one experience where I went through the process, and as the emotions came to the forefront, I started crying and had a huge emotional release. A weight was lifted from me and I felt amazing. What was initially a 10 out of 10 on the emotional pain scale, after the first time of letting go, it was a 7. After another letting go session, it was a 4. Each time it became less and less until eventually, it came up and I was able to smile at it and it didn't have any emotional effect on me. I still remember what happened, but I have released the emotional response and moved on and it's no longer a story or self-belief that I buy into. Sometimes, it will be a one and done for some of the emotional responses you have. But if it comes back again, we repeat the process until we no longer have the heavy emotional response to the event, person, or situation.

Dr. David R. Hawkins wrote a wonderful book called *Letting Go.* In his book, he talks about the concept that thousands of thoughts and feelings make up an emotion. If you can lean into that emotion and let go, thousands of these thoughts and associated feelings will be addressed in that one sitting. Initially, this was too overwhelming for me. Instead, I started leaning into thoughts and their associated feelings and letting go of individual thoughts. I then addressed individual situations and individual people and before I knew it, I was in the habit of letting go. Dr. Hawkins says when you start letting go, you send signals to your body that you are in a letting go mode, and it becomes much easier to continue letting go. After having done this many times, I have to say that I agree. The first few times were hard, but it becomes easier each time. Now when an emotion comes up, it isn't so overwhelming and I am able to work on letting go of that emotion.

There are still some times when a feeling of sadness comes over me, or I will be fearful of something or feel overwhelmed. When this happens, I look to the why. I try to find the root cause of why this emotion is coming up. Often it is one of three things. Either I am reliving an event from the past, I am comparing myself to someone, or I am going into an unknown situation and I can't control the outcome and all of its variables and I get overwhelmed. Once I realize I am out of present moment, I bring awareness to the situation. Then I am able to dive into what is taking me to the past, or future. I am able to sit with it, while leaning in and letting go.

As we work through these emotional experiences, I want to underscore that I am not saying we forget the past or to act as if something didn't happen. As stated earlier, I had metastatic testicular cancer at 18. I knew that I would get through it and come out on the other side, but with that experience, I definitely had emotional responses that I pushed down. Many were unconsciously repressed, and when they came up, I was taken aback. It was so many years ago, but as they were repressed without me realizing it, hiding in plain sight. By leaning in and letting go, I was able to address the emotions behind the experience, and it didn't negate having cancer, which ultimately changed my life for the better. It didn't negate that I am a survivor, and it was part of the motivation of why I went into the healthcare field to become a physician assistant. In fact, it helped me look back at that time in my life as something that built so much character that I carry to this day. I also know as important as it was in my timeline, it is but one of many aspects of who I am. I released the emotional baggage I was carrying while still knowing that the experience of having cancer and surviving is still a part of my journey.

Surrender and lean in & let go are related concepts. Many people would say they are the same, and that is fine. To me, I separate them because I utilize them differently. Once you read each chapter, you may decide for yourself if in fact they are different concepts or the same. To me, surrender is dropping the oars of the rowboat and becoming the flow of the water, going along with the current. It is surrendering control. I stop trying to control everything or stop resisting what is. I am surrendering to a higher power outside of and beyond me, to God, to the universe, spirit, energy, or to nature. When I surrender, I am saying, "This is too much for me. I am going to relinquish control. I am getting out of the boat and I am going to be the water. Current, take me where you will, as I know this is beyond me and all will be ok."

The concept of Lean In & Let Go helps me more when I have emotional blocks. It's when I have emotional baggage that is affecting my daily life. Yes, I can surrender to this, but it feels too passive for me. When I lean in & let go, I am actively engaged in the process. I have a part to play. That part is to sit with the discomfort and breath through it.

The two concepts are so related, that you may say surrender and then end up letting go. Or you may try to let go and do so by surrendering to a higher power. There is no right or wrong way to surrender or let go. The most important thing is that you are moving forward!

Note: This concept asks you to sit with your thoughts and emotions, and it may cause anxiety or other intense emotions when bringing up past feelings and experiences. If it is too much for you, stop. Some traumatic life experiences need a qualified medical professional to deal with trauma responses, and this book is merely a guide. It is not a substitute for professional help. If you are suffering from a traumatic experience and need professional help, see the "Additional Resources" section at the end of the book, knowing that asking for help is a sign of strength!

Lean-In and Let Go:

When a thought, feeling, emotion or limiting self-beliefs comes on and begins to overwhelm, become aware of this feeling. Sadness, anger, uneasiness, fear and anxiety are some of the feelings that commonly come up when we are associated with an emotional response. When this occurs, we want to become aware that it is happening. This is usually the most challenging part, because we are so used to avoiding, numbing or redirecting when this occurs. When you become aware of what you have been holding onto, consciously or unconsciously, engage in the process below.

To make it easier and have a quick win, start with something small or simple that is easier to sit through and release. Starting with the most traumatic experience of your life is not the way to go about this. Become fully aware and open, with self-compassion, self-love and self-forgiveness at the forefront.

Find a place to sit. Plant your feet firmly on the floor to help ground yourself. This was very helpful for me in the beginning so I knew I was in a safe position and less vulnerable. The goal is for you to feel safe in your current environment (though your thoughts may be screaming out, you know you are physically safe).

Next, lean in, mentally and physically. Mentally, by allowing yourself to have the feeling/emotion without judgment or criticism or condemnation of it. Physically, by leaning forward while sitting. This sends a signal to self that you are in this to work through this and you are not going anywhere.

Bring awareness to the breath and continue breathing while sitting with the feeling/emotion. Sit in the present moment, relinquishing attachment and identification to the feeling/emotion.

Continue to breath, letting the feeling or emotion come to the surface and feel it fully. Observe any tightness in our chest. Observe the story being told and just sit there without judging or rating it as good, bad or other. When it feels uncomfortable, continue to breathe through the feeling/emotion, instead of trying to push it away or resisting it. Stay present.

Breathing in and out, say to yourself, "I am and always will be ok". Then exhale saying, "I let go of identification with this (emotional response)". If it is too overwhelming, stop and get help. But ideally, the goal is to stay with the process instead of running or numbing or distracting ourselves from feeling the discomfort of what is being released.

Give yourself permission to break any attachment you have with the story around the emotion.

While sitting and leaning in, continue to breathe; feeling the pain, anxiety and anguish of what's going through your mind without avoiding, changing, repressing or suppressing the thought, feeling or emotion.

Visualize the release of the feeling/emotion. I often picture myself as the ocean and as the waves crash, these feeling/emotions are released from me.

Remember: However, this felt going in, it is going to feel the same coming out. The goal is to let it come to the surface without any interference other than feeling the intensity of the feeling, knowing this intensity will pass!

You may have anger, frustration and tears. That's ok! In my meditation practice, we say "Better Out Than In" or BOTI as I call it.

Continue experiencing the uncomfortable feeling and continue to breathe through it, sitting in the present moment without judging as good vs bad, right vs wrong saying, "I am aware this is hard and painful and I am ok. I keep my focus on this and I will get through this."

Usually around 3-5 minutes, maybe shorter, maybe longer, you will suddenly feel the sensation lessen. It starts to melt away. The energy changes, and it has passed. You feel different. A weight has been lifted, and you are healing. You have just let go and released trapped energy!

Again, if this is too much for you, and some trauma is, please see the "Additional Resources" section to seek professional help as you do not need to do this alone.

11

Forgiveness

I forgive for my sake, and I am all the stronger for it!

The concept of forgiveness can be a challenging one for many people. I know it was for me. The person we don't want to forgive from that situation we are holding onto can become so hardwired in our mind that we don't even realize we are carrying the anger and frustration from this past event. When we are unaware, at times going through life as if we are sleepwalking, we don't even realize that we are carrying a heavy emotional burden that affects us in our daily lives. It can also affect those around us due to the emotional energy we have for what happened. This is why I recommend forgiveness, if and when you want to, on your own terms.

Forgiveness is the act of opening your heart and mind, letting go of frustration, hatred, anger and/or resentment towards self, another person or a situation, and finding peace in the present moment. In practice, it is usually thought of as, "I forgive you," but it's just as important to say, "I forgive myself" or "I forgive and let go of what happened." It does not mean we approve of or condone the behavior or situation that occurred, but it allows us to move on for our sake, releasing the emotional burden we are carrying. Forgiveness is not about the other person, though at times it can be. When you forgive, it is to support yourself.

When I forgive, I am able to let go of anger, hatred, resentment and other negative emotions that weigh me down. I become freer and the load is lightened. "Forgiveness is the gift you give yourself," as I once heard. Forgiveness isn't a sign of weakness, but a sign of strength; a sign of self-empowerment. It also doesn't mean that what happened was ok. Forgiveness doesn't condone what happened. It's the opposite. It's acknowledging that it happened. Forgiveness allows us to lean into the feeling, accept that it happened and that it's now over, and release the emotional energy behind it.

In one experience I had, forgiveness took the edge off the pain from the anger and resentment I had for someone who harassed me all throughout their time as my boss at a job I once held. To be honest, both of us were unaware. As we were unaware, we were both consumed by our egos, associated as one with them. I viewed this person as someone who was manipulative and emotionally abusive because they did in fact abuse their authority. But I also played a part. As I was unaware and associated with my ego, I bought into their antics. I personalized what was happening and became a victim and a martyr. In doing that, I lost my inherent worth and power to set an intention and perform next right action. I gave them my priceless energy and believed what they said about me and resented how they treated not only me, but others as well. Now that I am aware, it all makes sense in hindsight, but in the moment, it was a terrible experience for me. And while it makes sense, forgiving them doesn't excuse or condone their behavior, but it is in the past, it is over with, so I forgive for me so that I may move on and be free of the heavy emotional burden associated with them.

One day when I was working for them, they escalated a situation and made me the fall person for something that didn't warrant any blame. Their behavior was so out of proportion to what was going on, and I personalized what was happening so intensely, that I had a spontaneous nose bleed because my blood pressure was so high. The physical effects of the stress in the situation were so intense that my body was screaming out. As I started creating the framework that would become Possley's Paradigm, I hit a wall with this person when I got to the concept of forgiveness. I said to myself, "Why would I forgive that piece of garbage? They were such a monster!" As you can see, based on my assessment of them, I was heavily associated with my ego as well, playing the victim and making them a "piece of garbage."

As time when on, I was able to realize this person was heavily identified with their fear-bed ego and were overcompensating. They loved the power they had over others and wanted their subordinates to know it. This person was lashing out with their egoic pain and projected it onto me and others, but I wasn't aware of this at the time, so I took it on and internalized and made it my problem when it wasn't. It did not make their actions correct in any way, but when I forgave them, I took my energy back from them by forgiving and letting go.

I still have vivid memories of them, but now, instead of my ego making them into a monster in my memory, they are a human who is hurting like many of us and I do not think they are a monster or garbage at all. I know that was my ego acting out just like their ego is acting out. Their actions were not warranted or right in any way, but I let go of my emotional connection to them and now I wish them well. I let go of the intense emotional energy I was giving to the situation, and now my priceless energy is for me, as it should always be. In my forgiving, I haven't forgotten what happened, I don't condone the behavior, and it took time and distance from this person to reach this point.

While forgiveness didn't happen in the moment, a couple of years later, with space and a new perspective, I was able to forgive and move on. And when I forgave them, I underscore that it wasn't for them—*it was for me*. I was the only one who was still hurting and carrying the heavy emotional baggage of the experience. By forgiving them, I healed myself. I didn't want to hold onto the anger anymore, and for me, I knew it was time to let go. I didn't need to confront them. I didn't need them to know I forgave them. That wasn't the point. The point was for me to let go. This was for my own self-liberation.

Additionally, we are taught from a young age to "forgive and forget." That puts immense pressure on a person if they can't forgive, let alone forget. I don't believe in the forget aspect. As humans, we are wired to have memories of significant events, and emotional events create stronger memories. To say, "forgive and forget," so casually creates a second victim for the person who cannot forgive, let along forget and move on. The person who is struggling to move on, now has another burden. "What's wrong with me that I refuse to forgive and forget?" I am here to say nothing is wrong with you. We choose to be kind to ourselves, having self-compassion, and take small steps to success. We also know we will not likely forget, but the emotional charge has lessened so it no longer has the same effect on us.

> I forgive for me, on my terms, if and when I am ready to, so I can let go of the emotional burden I have been carrying. Forgiving doesn't condone what happened and it doesn't mean I forget what happened. Forgiveness allows me to let go of anger and resentment, thus allowing me to live my life more fully.

You decide if and when you will forgive. It is a highly personal journey that is on your terms. I cannot say to someone, "You must forgive." I don't know the history and experience they are having. Some people feel some things are too egregious to ever forgive. I get that. For me, the concept of forgiveness has been immensely powerful on my journey, so to make it easier, I recommend people forgive after some time has elapsed, after they have awareness and understanding, and if they decide they want to forgive; knowing it doesn't make what happened ok, but it lets them let go of the heavy boulder of emotional energy they are carrying. And if you decide you can't or don't want to forgive, that's ok. Consider finding a way to release the energy you are carrying through the lean in and let go technique, as that may be easier in the beginning.

I once heard an expression, attributed to Buddha, that anger is like holding onto a hot coal and expecting the other person to get burned. We are hurt not for having our anger, but rather we are hurt by holding onto it. Instead of holding onto it, we let it go, if and when we are ready, through the act of forgiveness.

There are many situations that you could list and say to me, "You expect me to forgive them?" My answer would be, "Absolutely not. You forgive on your terms if and when you are ready." Time is a huge factor in being able to forgive. An incident from last week versus 3 years ago is a drastically different situation when it comes to forgiveness. You decide when you are ready, knowing that forgiveness doesn't erase the past, but it helps us release our grip on it so we can move forward.

A situation arose years ago where I felt my father was slighted by someone near and dear to him. When the "offending" person died, my anger continued. I couldn't get over the slight that occurred to my dad, and I carried the anger with me for years. One day, I again erupted in anger. My ego loved that. The soapbox my egoic self enjoyed getting on was ready and waiting for me. My sister Sherry, who has always loved me and supported me unconditionally, looked over and said in the most supportive way, "You are so angry at something that happened so long ago. You are holding onto this anger and it's only hurting you now." In that moment, a light bulb went off. She was right and I was speechless. I wasn't even aware of how hardwired this belief was in my mind. She was my awareness, and years after the incident, I was ready to let go and forgive. I even smiled at the thought of the person who had passed, and now had pleasant memories and was able to smile.

When the situation occurred years prior, forgiveness wasn't on my immediate radar and I was not ready to, nor would I forgive, so I held onto it and made it a story, wearing it as a badge of honor. No one could tell me otherwise. I wasn't ready to hear it until that moment with my sister. It is rarely possible in the moment for many people. But over time, through awareness and acceptance, and with surrender and letting go, we sometimes are able to reach a state of acceptance with what happened, and I was able to let go and forgive. The emotional weight I let go of that day was immense. That's why we forgive.

Forgiveness usually becomes easier once some time has elapsed, and using the concepts here, we learn that the anger can subside over time if we allow it, feeling the emotion and letting it pass, instead of holding onto it and storing it. It's in this space that there is room to start the forgiveness process. I always remind myself of what my sister taught me. My anger only hurts me. It prevents me from living. It keeps me small and fearful; resentful and angry at the world, so much to the point that I stop living. I lived in anger over the past and worried so much about the future, that I was missing out on the beauty of present moment and those around me. And that is why we forgive when we are ready to.

I also find it easier to forgive when I start with something small. Start with forgiving yourself and move outward from there. When we practice forgiveness with the small stuff, it's easier and we create wins along the way. This builds the muscle and it becomes easier over time to forgive the bigger stuff. When we start to forgive the small stuff in everyday life, over time, this helps us with the bigger stuff.

Think of the person who cut you off when you were driving. Do you think they set out with an intention to upset you when they left their house this morning? Very unlikely. What if they were running late for an important job interview, or rushing to the hospital to see a sick friend. There are so many scenarios we can create, but the one we often go to is, "that idiot cut me off," and we end up personalizing something that isn't personal. When we can forgive and let go in those small moments, we continue to build that muscle and forgiveness becomes easier. It doesn't mean we like that we got cut off, and it doesn't mean we don't feel frustration. We will likely have strong feelings in the moment, but since we are aware and no longer sleepwalking through life, the strong feelings pass more easily as we aren't storing them. We aren't holding onto the driver who cut us off when we walk into work. We don't set our day based on this incident. It didn't happen to us, it just happened and we were there.

And let's say the driver did cut you off intentionally. Over time as we apply this concept of forgiveness and the other concepts of the paradigm, we can begin to understand that we all make mistakes. We have compassion for the driver in their humanness, which in turn allows us to have compassion for ourselves in our humanness. We see, understand and appreciate our limitations based on many experiences. When we can forgive that driver, choosing to not hold onto the feelings of anger and frustration, we can allow ourselves to be human and accept our own imperfections. This allows us to move towards self-forgiveness.

I have a friend who cannot forgive themselves for their past. It breaks my heart to see, but I know they are on their own journey. They are facing their past with eyes wide open and working on themselves, so I know they will get to the point of having self-compassion and being able to forgive. In the meantime, I support them as able and reassure them that it's ok, telling them to forgive themselves for the imperfections they see that make them human. They are holding onto the stories of their past because they have become so identified as one with them. The ego has a solid grip, constantly reminding them of how "bad" they were. I was there in their life, and I know this person. They weren't "bad" at all. They were human and were always doing their best. But when the ego has its grip and when you think you are your thoughts, it's hard to separate from them, which is why I created this paradigm, so we can understand that our past actions don't define our worth today. I tell this friend to have self-compassion, and to be open to the idea of forgiving themselves in time.

We also practice forgiveness when our expectations aren't met. I come to the table as I am, but if I am expected to be perfect, or have all the answers, or have an expectation to be super-human, then I am bound to fail. Through forgiveness, we can see other's humanness and stop putting people on pedestals, only to be disappointed at a later time as we gleefully shove them off the pedestal when they make a mistake. We forgive them and accept what is, was or will be. We see their humanness in our humanness. We work towards awakening ourselves from the sleepwalking state so that others may awaken as well.

Remember, forgiveness is a process, and as such, it may come in stages. It may not be immediate. You may not be ready to forgive just yet. Be patient and compassionate with yourself. And you may need to have conditions around it. The goal is to protect our emotional well-being, and that may mean, not having the person we forgive in our life. Some people are not aware and as I've said, they go through life sleepwalking. I was sleepwalking myself, but now that I am aware, I see things differently. The concept of forgiveness can be a challenge if the other person you want to forgive is sleepwalking, or not aware themselves. Worse yet, they could be someone in a friendship circle or a family member. These are challenging situations that are unique and not a one size fits all model. We may have to quit our job, create distance or set boundaries from that friend or family member. The situation with my boss was a challenge until thankfully they quite and I was given the space I needed. In hindsight, I stayed in a situation when I should have looked for a job elsewhere, but again, I wasn't aware at the time. In hindsight, I would have handled it different, but instead of focusing on that, I have self-compassion, knowing I did the best at the time. I sit in acceptance knowing what happened, happened. It's uncomfortable, but I stopped fighting what was.

When we forgive, we find self-liberation. We are no longer carrying a burden that only affects us. And forgiving doesn't mean we always forgive in the moment. As I said earlier, time heals many emotional wounds making it easier to for us to forgive weeks, months or years later. And forgiveness is not the same as reconciliation. As discussed, we forgive for ourselves, and that doesn't mean bringing someone back into our life. We may need to keep a clear boundary for a myriad of reasons, and that is ok. This is where we can forgive ourselves. We may feel we need to forgive, forget and bring someone back into our lives, but if they are not aware and not on a journey of improvement, you may need to go in a different direction and separate from that person in the short term or long term. With your newfound awareness, you decide next steps.

You do this by first showing respect to self, then outwardly as you show respect to others. And respect to others doesn't mean being a yes-person or a doormat. Clear, healthy boundaries are tough. I think of boundaries in two ways. One, I am respecting myself by setting boundaries. Two, I respect you by setting boundaries. Boundaries may mean keeping someone out of my life, or it can mean I want you in my life, but here are the boundaries, or guardrails, to keeping this a healthy relationship. This isn't always easy, but when you respect yourself and others, and start small, it will get easier over time. Yes, you may lose people close to you, and this can be a challenge, but we go back to sitting in acceptance of what is, was or will be. We do our best in the present to forgive, set boundaries as a form of love and self-respect, while finding contentment in the present moment.

In writing this chapter on forgiveness, I know I have been repetitive. It's intentional, because I, along with many others, struggle with this concept. Likewise, to close out this chapter, I underscore that we forgive for ourselves, so we no longer have to carry the emotional burden. We forgive if and when we want to, on our terms, knowing that something that happened recently versus something that happened years ago may perhaps be viewed differently. It may be easier to forgive for something from several years ago versus something that happened last week, or not. There are no clear rules here. If there's a way you can release the emotional burden without forgiving, that's great—then release it. If you can't, be ok with that as well. You tried! Forgiveness is but one step and you may feel it may not be time to forgive based on what happened, and that's ok. If you can't forgive what happened, then have self-compassion and empathy for yourself and find other ways to release the emotional energy so you don't have to carry the burden.

We forgive if and when we want to, on our terms, knowing it is a sign of strength, knowing it takes inner-courage to do so, and that it does not condone what happened. Forgiveness doesn't assume reconciliation, as we may need to put up healthy boundaries as a sign of respect for self and other. Forgiveness means releasing the emotional attachment to the situation and deciding that it no longer has the power to control our present mood, our actions or our self-worth.

We may never forget what happened, but we can choose to be free from the anger, pain or resentment associated with that event. By forgiving, we are not being passive or resigned; rather, we are strong, not weak, as we consciously choose a path of healing and liberation, knowing forgiveness is a journey. When we forgive on our terms, we reclaim our power from the past. Anger, resentment and pain can consume our energy, distracting us from the present moment and limiting our potential for happiness and fulfillment. Through forgiveness, we take back that power and channel it into living fully in the here and now. Forgiving can be hard when we live in what we "should" be doing or what "should" have happened. When we stop "should" thinking, we make space for the forgiveness journey to unfold naturally, knowing that forgiveness also happens in its own time.

Practicing Forgiveness:

I bring my awareness to past situations that I may not even realize I am holding onto. Who or what angers me and why? Does it matter anymore? Can I let it go? Make a list of all the people who have wronged you in some way and see if there's an easy person or situation to forgive. Create an easy win and start building the forgiveness muscle.

I then work towards accepting what happened, which doesn't mean I like what happened. Sit in the discomfort and accept what was. Acceptance doesn't mean I approve of or condone what happened. I am aware I cannot change what happened and forgiveness does not condone what happened or make what happened ok.

I am aware I may never forget, because the brain stores emotional memories more vividly.

I sit and lean-in (like the Lean In & Let Go technique). I feel the discomfort and as I breathe through it, I begin to let go and move towards forgiving the person. This may have to happen over several sessions, which is why I recommend you work on forgiving someone for something small that isn't as emotionally triggering.

Forgiveness for small things will become easy over time. Starting small for me was easier instead of tackling a huge mountain. There's no right or wrong way to start. Just start if and when you are ready.

Continue to breathe, saying to yourself, "I let go of anger and fear and hatred and resentment. I let go for me. I forgive so that I may let go of the emotional weight I have been carrying, and I come back to a place where I can forgive. What happened/what they did was not right, but it was in the past and I want to move on for me. I want to be free of this heavy load of anger and hatred and frustration."

As you continue to forgive yourself and others, you will likely start setting boundaries and start saying no. This is great progress. It means you are putting yourself in situations to succeed. Some people, including family, won't understand this. That is ok.

I forgive for me because I am worth it!

12

Affirmations & Gratitude

I am beautiful, I am strong, I am worth it, I am enough!

A ffirmations and gratitude are what I call *mindset shifters*. When I am
heavily associated with and identified as my thoughts, feelings, and emotions, believing what they say about me and the world around me, being
emotionally dragged down by them, I can read a simple affirmation statement
or write out what I am grateful for, and it takes the edge off and helps me
identify with True Self. I read my affirmation statement daily, right when I get
up, and right before I go to bed. In my daily journal, I have a gratitude section.
This is for the times when I know I have a figurative bag of silver coins, but all I
can see is the tarnish, meaning I am not seeing what I really have because I am
coming from a place of lack or scarcity, instead of coming from an abundance
mindset. It is during these times that I use affirmations and gratitude to help
shift my mindset out of lack and scarcity and into one of plentiful abundance.

In using affirmations and gratitude, I am not trying to create a mood. My
affirmations are not, "I am happy" or "I am not angry." My gratitude exercises
are not, "I should be happy because I have a roof over my head." This is trying
to create a mood that I am not feeling naturally, hence the term mood-making.
With affirmations and gratitude, we are not trying to change our mood or create
a mood that we aren't feeling. We allow ourselves to feel the feelings we are
having. Instead of being tethered to and identifying as one with our feelings
and going down the proverbial rabbit hole of gloom and doom, we let our
feelings come up while reminding ourselves of the other positive aspects of
our life that can be overshadowed when we are heavily associated with our
negative thoughts, feelings and emotions.

We are trying to shift our mindset to better align with True Self. There have
been times I have said my affirmations and done my gratitude exercises and
still felt sad. It is ok to feel the sadness. It's an emotion that may be warranted.

When I am feeling sad, I can say an affirmation or do a gratitude exercise and it takes the edge off, preventing me from spiraling into association with my ego.

Another example of this can be when I am angry. I used to say to myself, "I am not angry," but I was! I would try to pretend I wasn't because anger is viewed as a bad or negative emotion. Now I've grown to appreciate my anger as it's a yellow caution flag. My anger is alerting me that something is going on inside me. It is stored emotional energy that is being triggered and activated from my past. I don't try to change my anger to happiness, but I do look at the root cause to understand the why. I don't have an affirmation that says, "I won't get angry anymore." That just doesn't make sense. Anger is an emotion and we have it for a reason. Just know the why behind it instead of trying to make of mood of it into something it is not. As long as your affirmations avoid creating a false mood and avoid changing an emotion to 'put on a good face', that is fine.

The same is true for gratitude. When I am feeling down or things feel over-whelming, I can turn to gratitude to shift my mindset so I don't get bogged down by negative, ruminating thinking patterns. If I didn't get the promotion I wanted, it doesn't mean I don't allow myself to feel the disappointment. But instead of associating as one with the disappointment, I can be grateful for my current job, and the benefits I have. I can be grateful for my skill set, and use this knowledge to work towards improving my skills so I can apply for the next promotion. Affirmations and gratitude keep me in the game, keep me in present moment, bringing awareness to the idea that while I will always have thoughts, feelings and emotions, I am separate from them. Affirmations and gratitude remind me that what happened has happened, and I can sit in acceptance of that knowing that I am not a victim or a martyr, while I continue to feel my feelings instead of storing them. I can let my feelings come up, letting them pass, and use affirmations and gratitude to shift into an abundance mindset. This is empowering!

Affirmations and gratitude shift our mindset from a place of lack and scarcity to a mindset of plentiful abundance!

Affirmations

Affirmations are empowering statements which help support a more positive mindset, helping counteract negative self-talk. This can lead to improved self-confidence, an increase in motivation and promote an improved sense of self and well-being.

My affirmations are always positively worded. I avoid works like can't, don't, won't, shouldn't, etc. They all come from an "I can", "I will", "I am" framework, which then become foundational and powerful statements to ground me. The affirmation I use the most is, "I am beautiful, I am strong, I am worth it, I am enough!"

- "I am beautiful," because as True Self, free of egoic association, we are all shining examples of beauty. We are not comparing ourselves to someone else or to society's standards of beauty. We are beautiful in our own right.

- "I am strong," because if I woke up today, that means I am strong. I may not feel it or perceive it, but it's true! Did I get out of bed? Did I get dressed? If I can walk or run or talk or text, then I am blessed and strong.

- "I am worth it," because I am here and there are no mistakes in that. The odds of you being here on earth are estimated at 1 in 400 trillion, with some estimating even greater odds. For so long, my worth was based in ego, which based my worth on what I looked like, sounded like, what job I had, where I lived, etc. All fleeting externals. When my worth aligns with True Self, knowing I beat the odds, I have my worth from within.

- And last but not least, "I am enough." I don't need someone's approval or love or a new car or a new house to be enough. It's fine to have the new car and nice job, but our sense of self-worth is not based on those things. Just by being born and being alive, I AM ENOUGH! That absolute is already within me.

By working through the paradigm and saying this (or your own) affirmation daily, we start to uncover years of socialized behaviors that have sent us the message that I need "you and your approval" to be complete. That I need to look, act and sound like you to fit in. That happiness is found external to me instead of internally from within. This is another game-changer in life when we start to realize that our true power lies within. That we are beautiful, we are strong, we are worth it, and we are enough without external validation.

I once heard the expression, "Whether you think you can or you can't, you are correct." How true that is! Affirmations help confront negative thinking and turn it around to a positive. Instead of coming from an "I can't," I change it to an "I can" or "I will try" or "this may be a challenge but I will have fun trying regardless of the outcome." I have written many affirmation statements for friends and family. The focus being on healing the body, and focusing on what the person can do and what they want to do, as opposed to focusing on what they can't do, the negative, the scarcity aspect. Contentment must come from within. It's not "over there" and it's not a destination, and affirmations reflect that.

Did I work hard and make a salary that allowed me to live my life more easily, and is that ok? Absolutely! To deny that would be insincere. And with that being said, for many years, with all I had, I was still unhappy and miserable be-cause I was trying to find my happiness and fulfillment from outside of myself. The money didn't bring me happiness, because that is what I call "destination happiness", and it was always fleeting. Destination happiness always lies in the future. "I'll be happy when I make six figures, have a spouse, have a vacation home, or [insert statement]." Instead of making these future statements, we turn inward, finding our contentment and happiness from within. These future declarations of happiness keep our happiness elusive and one step away from us. If I say, "I'll finally be happy when I retire," yet I don't retire for another 10 years, where does my happiness lie? Where do I find my contentment? I can't find it from you or from the items I own as those are fleeting. Therefore, I learn to find my contentment from within. When I do this, I have contentment as a foundation. There will be days where I am happy, sad, angry, joyous or resentful to name a few emotions. Those emotions will come and go, but when I have inner-contentment as my foundation, I am the lighthouse that can weather the storm. That's what the paradigm is all about.

I've seen so many, including myself, achieve wealth and luxuries, as well as fitness and weight loss, and still end up feeling unhappy and unfulfilled. When this happened to me, it felt even worse, because now I had everything I'd ever wanted, but I still felt empty. Then it became, "Now what am I supposed to do? I have everything I've ever wanted and I still feel lost, empty and hopeless" because happiness and contentment were a destination. I was looking outside of myself instead of looking from within.

The paradigm helps you find happiness and fulfillment within, in the here and now, the present moment, with your current living situation and financial resources, current relationship status, etc. Am I knocking wealth or criticizing health and fitness? No! There is nothing wrong with having wealth and great fitness. It is a great idea to set goals for ourselves, to achieve what we want to achieve. But our inner contentment is not a "destination" to be achieved. It is not from a fleeting external source, like age, beauty, a job title or money. These all come and go, but when you have contentment and fulfillment from within, instead of from over there, it isn't fleeting and will always be there.

There is a caveat I want to make about affirmations. I've seen many people talk of affirmations, to me, similar to manifesting, for wealth creation. While I need money to live, I caution people to think that money & wealth will bring happiness. My affirmations have nothing to do with making millions. My affirmations have to do with helping millions. That is my wealth, so be aware that the goal is to find our inner contentment, and all the money in the world cannot buy you that! Is it ok to want the promotion or to want that raise, to get paid your worth for the work you are doing? Yes! Just be aware of both sides of the coin!

Affirmations:

Have your affirmations come from a positive & inspiring place of "I am," "I can," "I will," etc.

Avoid using negative words like can't, won't, don't, should, shouldn't, etc. and avoid "mood making."

Not sure what affirmations to start with? Use The Paradigm Affirmation: *I am Beautiful! I am Strong! I am Worth It! I am Enough!*

You can also have other affirmations that change more frequently, based on a current challenge or issue that I want to work through: "I can do this." "I can achieve this." "This may be tough, but I can do it!"

Write your affirmations down on paper and tape them to your bathroom mirror or your work computer as a reminder to say them morning and night. Find a piece of paper and write an affirmation statement now.

Gratitude gives us the perspective that makes every day
moments extraordinary!

Gratitude

Gratitude is appreciation for the good you already have in your life, appreciation for what you and others have, and appreciation for the good going on in the world around you. Gratitude can be said verbally, mentally or be written out for you to look at when you want to. Practicing gratitude, whether in thought, spoken or written down, acknowledges and brings to the forefront of mind all the good things that are going on around you. It does not mean everything is always great and fine, but it allows a person to see that good is happening around them. Gratitude can also help people move from a place of scarcity, lack and not enough (fear-based emotions of the small self ego), to a place of abundance, that there is in fact enough (True Self). It can also help people see and feel the interconnectedness of the world, making people more compassionate towards self and others.

When I practice gratitude, I prefer to write it down. It gives me something to physically see and associate with. Thinking gratitude and saying what you are grateful for is fine, but for me, the physical aspect of writing the words down is more powerful for me.

The human experience, what we call life, is a journey of ups and downs. Staying in present moment with self-value and self-worth from within, instead of trying to find it outside of ourselves, can be tough at times. Gratitude exercises helped me refocus myself from a thought-driven reality to a present moment reality. I also try to get creative with my gratitude statements. When I first started writing what I am grateful for, it was always, "I am grateful for friends and family." While that is true, over the years, I've become much more granular. I will look at the day prior and find anything to be grateful for and write it down in a journal or on a scrap piece of paper that I carry with me throughout each day. One day, I was feeling off and I was trying to find gratitude in every minute thing around me and anything & everything that came to mind. This is what I wrote:

I am grateful that I woke up this morning. I am grateful that I can see, hear, taste, touch, smell and feel. I am grateful for everything around me: I am grateful for sidewalks and elevators. I am grateful for wheelchairs and wheelchair ramps/accessible entrances for people; I am grateful for computers and the internet. I am grateful for this food on my plate. I am grateful for clothing and a roof over my head. I am grateful for the people who helped harvest and prepare the food on my plate, made my clothing and built my housing. I am grateful for indoor plumbing, I am grateful for running water; I am grateful for heating and cooling; I am grateful for my refrigerator; I'm grateful for beaches and vacations, cable TV, gyms, yoga, meditation, tax refunds, bar code scanning, and cell phone technology.

Yes, every random thing made it to my list that day, and the list could have gone on and on, but I started smiling at the randomness of what came to mind. Anything I could think of that day went on my gratitude list. It's your list so you make it as specific as you want. Anything you can think of, write down and give gratitude.

Other times, as soon as I open my eyes in the morning, I will whisper the word "gratitude" to myself 10 or more times just to engage that part of me that may have forgot there is a lot of good going on in my world that I can be in appreciation of. It doesn't mean I can't have a bad day; it just softens the edge of the sword so it's not as painful. It decreases the likelihood that my ego will take over and go into a rabbit hole of all that is going wrong. I still allow myself to have my feelings. Gratitude just helps me keep things in perspective. Does it hurt to be fired? To suffer a breakup? To not get the promotion? Absolutely! But we can soften the blow by looking at what we do have in our lives through the lens of gratitude. The goal of gratitude exercises is to shift your mindset and thinking, so you can come from a place of positivity and abundance while still having all of your feelings and emotions; you just don't want to buy into the egoic thoughts and story behind the feelings and emotions.

Gratitude exercises help shift your thinking into abundance. When I have a negative mindset with negative thinking, I take 5 minutes and write down everything I can think of to be grateful for. It brings me back to an abundance mindset and the negative dark cloud moves off into the distance again. You may not feel the benefits of writing and reading a daily affirmation or practicing gratitude daily immediately, but try practicing affirmations and gratitude for one week and see how much of an improvement you feel in your life. It's guaranteed!

Not sure what to be grateful for? Try being grateful for each of your senses: "I am grateful that I can see and read, that I can touch and feel, smell, hear and taste; grateful that I can run, walk, or ride a bike." If you don't have all your senses, or you are not able to do some of those things, then be grateful for what you can still do.

One day I was talking to my dad. He's in his 80's and doesn't feel like he used to. I told him that must be tough. I didn't negate anything he said. It is tough. Things have changed. His body and mind have aged. He started listing all the things he couldn't do and how this bothered him. I saw how down he was; his energy tanked. I asked him to list 3 things that he could do. He just looked at me and didn't know what to say. I asked, "Can you dress and feed yourself?" He said, "Yes." I asked, "Are you still independent living in this house with your wife?" He said, "Yes." I asked, "Are you able to raise your hands above your head, walk around on your own and see and hear what I'm saying?" He said, "Yes."

And then he just started smiling; his energy shifted almost immediately. I didn't negate that he misses the energy he used to have and that he misses riding on his motorcycle. I know how hard that is for him and I don't want to negate that. But I also wanted him to counter those statements to what he could do. He started laughing and it lessened the sting of not being able to ride his motorcycle anymore. He still wishes he could, and he is also grateful for what he can do, which elevated his mood and energy instantaneously. It's sometimes the simplest things to be grateful for that help the most.

This is what gratitude is all about. Remember that it's ok to have a bad day. It's ok to not feel your best. It's ok to have all of your emotions, especially the negative ones. When we are not feeling our best, that is when gratitude can help. Find something to be grateful for in that moment.

I once didn't get a job I knew I'd be perfect for. I wasn't devastated because I was doing gratitude the entire time. It was the first time I was up for a promotion where either outcome would be ok, because I had gratitude statements on either side of the outcome. I was initially disappointed in not getting the promotion, but it allowed me to do something so much better in the long run. I didn't know this at the time, but with the benefit of hindsight I can see this now. Gratitude helped soften the blow. That is how we can use gratitude in our daily lives.

Try it out right now! Write down three things you are grateful for and read it out loud to yourself morning and night. See how your week changes!

13

Action

The key to getting unstuck is to set an intention and perform next right action.

When I felt lost and *stuck inside my head*, so heavily identified as one with my thoughts, I was convinced I was broken. When I was associating as one with what my thoughts said about me and the world around me, I was unable to separate from the thoughts because I thought they were me. The thoughts would creep up out of nowhere and overtake me. I would sink so deep and so fast into an overwhelmed and lost state, further confirming the false belief that, "I am broken." It would be so bad at times that I wouldn't be able to get off the couch. I couldn't even pick up the phone to reach out and talk to someone because it was too hard and took too much energy. I was frozen and overwhelmed until one day, when a friend of mine told me *to set an intention and perform the next right action.* This became the key to my personal liberation and the final concept in Possley's Paradigm!

Next right action refers to the immediate next step you will perform. It's not about what you will do this afternoon, tomorrow or next week. It is the action you will perform in this *immediate* moment. It helps with the overwhelming feeling that is sometimes felt when getting unstuck from thought and trying to move into action. I visualize the intention portion as me looking to the left, knowing my negative, ruminating thoughts are on the right. When I look to the left, I see hope and opportunity. Then I perform the next right action and it helps get me unstuck. It's been so liberating for me. While it's the last concept in the paradigm we talk about, it's one of the most important for me as there are still times when I get stuck associated with my negative self-beliefs and thought patterns. By utilizing the paradigm as a roadmap and performing next right action, I am liberated.

One day when I felt overwhelmed and stuck, I knew my next right action was to meditate. I didn't know what I would do after that meditation, but I knew in that moment, my next right action would be to meditate, so I did. We all have a next right action, and we take it step by step, action by action.

Next right action may be turning off the TV. After that, the next right action may be getting up and putting shoes on, followed by the next right action of getting my jacket, then getting my keys, then walking out the door. Next right action can be taking a process such as leaving my apartment to walk around the block, and turning it into individual "next right action" steps.

My actions, however simple and small, would align with whatever my intention was. In the beginning, my intention was to get off the couch as I wanted to reengage with present moment living, enjoying life and living it to the fullest. At first, my next right actions were small. I'd literally turn my head to the side as if I was looking away from my thoughts. I would get off the couch and mindfully wash my hands, meaning, I paid attention to each and every step of the process (as mindful activities like washing your hands create space from those pervasive, ruminating thoughts) and felt what it was really like to wash my hands. In that one-minute exercise of washing my hands, I created space from identification with my thoughts. Then I would build on this space with additional next right actions.

The idea of setting an intention and performing next right action started to break the cycle of me feeling like I was emotionally stuck and unable to move off the couch. Mindfully washing my hands was the simplest task I could do, and when I did it mindfully, the completion of this next right action created a mini-win for me. From there, the next right action was to go outside and walk around the block, or go to the store. And at the store, if I felt overwhelmed, I would perform next right action and just get what I needed and leave. Sometimes the choices were too much and I wasn't in the head space to deal with it. Instead of shutting down, I purchased the few items I needed and would leave. Again, creating a mini-win. These small wins created space away from the ruminating thoughts and pervasive negative thinking that would take me down, and by completing the next right action, however small, I would find moments of joy and peace away from my false self-beliefs.

I felt the pleasure of the moment from next right action, and though I would often end up back on the couch, I knew I had achieved something small, yet important, because I chose action over the numbing inaction of mindlessly streaming and binging tv, often with a cocktail in my hand, my favorite numbing agent of choice. I still watch TV, but now I enjoy it and can walk away from it, as opposed to using it as a crutch or a thoughtless numbing device. It no longer has a hold over me. Next right action can be performed and I am no longer emotionally paralyzed with the inability to perform any action, because I just focus on the next right action.

> Next right action helps get us unstuck from the immobility we
> feel physically or emotionally when we are stuck associated or
> identified as one with our thoughts and belief patterns.

Sometimes when we are stuck associated with our ruminating thoughts, it is hard to think of a next right action. That is why I made a "life preserver" list of action items. It helped me think of all the things I could do to align with my intention. The list included everything from jumping jacks to calling a friend to walking around the block. The actions were simple, but in doing them, I aligned with my intention of getting unstuck. My list grew, and slowly over time, I realized more and more that when I get stuck associated with my thoughts, I now had an action plan I could reference. I restated my intention and referenced my action list to complete one or more next right actions. Each time, it created space for me from the intrusive, negative thoughts.

At first, the space created from my thoughts wouldn't last very long, but it was enough to give me hope to keep trying and continue creating mini-wins. I now had hope again, and with this hope, the momentum continued to carry me forward. Over time, the space created from my thoughts grew, and in performing next right action, I continued to strengthen the action muscles of living life instead of feeling like life was passing me by.

Mindfulness: Life at half speed!

Mindfulness is such a wonderful technique because we can easily bring it into our daily lives. When we are mindful in any situation, we bring our attention to what we are doing. By default, this pulls us out of association with our thoughts and brings us back to the present moment. One simple technique I often do is mindful handwashing, which I briefly discussed earlier. You can bring mindfulness to any task, and the easiest way to do that is to perform the task (handwashing, eating, getting dressed, brushing your teeth, texting, etc) at half-speed. When you perform any activity at half-speed, by default, you are bringing mindfulness into the activity because you are now thinking about the individual steps, instead of doing the activity on autopilot.

In mindful handwashing, we bring mindfulness to each and every step of the handwashing process. Handwashing is something we rarely think about. It's considered a one-step action by many. But when we break down each and every step and bring mindfulness to it, we are able to create that space to separate from our thoughts or our autopilot mode, by simply washing our hands. Pay attention to each step along the way. Be mindful as you are walking to the bathroom. What do you see along the way? Really pay attention to the cracks in the floor and the tile or paint on the walls as you walk to the bathroom. Bring attention to the door and door mechanism. As you walk to the sink, bring attention to the sink basin and the handle. What does the faucet feel like when you turn it on? What temperature of water do you use, and how does it feel? How does it feel when you put the soap on your hands and then massage the soap over your hands. How does the soap feel against your skin? Feel the water pass over your skin as you rinse the soap off. Bring attention to turning the faucet off, and feeling the towel or air dryer on your skin.

Mindfulness can also be applied to any task of your day. It can be done with showering, dressing, eating, walking, and commuting to work. I once read that if we tried to do everything at half-speed, we would automatically be in mindful awareness. This is the simplest and easiest action anyone can perform at any time. I tried texting at half-speed once. At first my brain resisted, but once I let go, I realized the joy of texting. Texting at half-speed was so calming. I wasn't so rushed. I was in the moment and enjoyed the process of texting. This was the easiest technique I'd ever heard of and practiced for bringing me into this mindful awareness, and it is at your disposal at any time.

The possibilities are endless. From dialing a phone for a conference call to making dinner, trying out activities at half-speed, if only for a moment, will create the space needed to bring you back to present moment. Since we know we can't stop the thoughts, we counteract them through action, action of any kind. Even if the action only gives a split second of attention away from the thought, it is enough to start separating from identification with the thoughts.

Mindless Scrolling

I have spent many late nights mindlessly scrolling social media. It felt fine until I realized my brain was so over-stimulated that I couldn't sleep. Additionally, I was left feeling worse after all of the doom-scrolling because I was comparing my lows to other people's highs. Quite often, on social media, while we feel we are connecting, we are actually disconnecting. It is such a passive action and often not an engaged next right action because there is no intention associated with it. We are looking at someone's highlight reel and comparing it to our lowlight reel, leaving us feeling more disconnected. Your ego will never have enough likes or followers. It will always want more. You want 100 followers and are excited with 50 likes, but all you can focus on is why you don't have more followers and likes. It's such a false narrative trying to feed the endless hunger of the ego and it is honestly futile. Instead, look at other actions on your list to help you out of that mindless scrolling rut and practice some gratitude for the followers and likes you have, instead of focusing on what you don't have.

Aligned with next right action, if I do find myself scrolling, I set guardrails around it, in how much time I allow myself to scroll and also in the content I let myself watch. I curate my feed so it only shows nature and positive, uplifting stories. Politics and people having breakdowns in public are not healthy entertainment for me, so I choose what makes me feel good. Additionally, in a 24/7 news cycle with people yelling and screaming at the other side as well as never ending social media content, we are dividing ourselves based on opinions and false stories, statements and claims. I choose to actively turn away from this for my mental health and well-being. Be intentional with what you consume and how you consume it!

I got stuck one night in a social media reel rabbit hole and 6 hours later, it was 4 am and I didn't sleep at all. My brain felt electrified in a bad way. I vowed to never do that again. But guess what? I did it again. Not until 4 am, but it was so easy to mentally check out and get hooked. This time however, I curated the most positive feed of animals and nature, kids laughing and positivity that I could. I don't let negativity in my feed and I've unfollowed negative feeds as needed. I also set a time limit, and when I am mindlessly scrolling, I'll sometimes ask myself, "What I am avoiding?" Then I come back to the paradigm to address the underlying issue. While I still enjoy some social media scrolling, I bring mindfulness to it and cap at a certain time limit, trying my best to avoid it anytime close to bedtime.

And along the same lines are current events and the 24/7 news cycle. Once or twice a week I will scroll a news app's headlines and read a few news articles. While I want to be knowledgeable about current events, I know the stories are often not presented in a way that is to inform me, but to spread fear. So many stories are negative and based out of fear which the ego loves. Very few stories are uniting people or sharing the good in the world that is happening, so they won't be read by me, and I am better for it. I am aware of what is going on in the world, but I am not paralyzed by it. I also see all the good that is going on in the world. What we attend to grows, and I want to attend to the idea of bringing people together instead of dividing us through opinions (which always change over time) and biased stories. There is so more that unites us than divides us and we just need to go beyond the surface of the ego's fear with its judgments, ratings and comparisons and see that as True Self, we are all very much alike.

Amygdala Hijack

Note: My experience and take on amygdala hijack is my own interpretation of the experience and what I learned after. It is not professional medical advice. I bring up amygdala hijack in the action section because it would occur quite often and would sometimes paralyze me throughout my career without me knowing what it was. Once I knew what it was, I was better able to get out of a hijack moment through one or two simple actions, and so I share in hopes it can help. When in amygdala hijack, we are not thinking rationally and are out of mindful awareness and next right action may not feel within reach, but in fact it can be through next right action. The amygdala is involved with fear and anxiety, so if you feel you have an untreated anxiety or panic disorder, please see the Additional Resources section as this book is no substitute for professional medical help.

Before I knew what amygdala hijack was, I often felt paralyzed in certain work and social situations where I felt like my brain went into a hyperactive over-drive, and I would just shut down. I never knew what it was, but I knew what it felt like. Years ago, I had a very challenging boss. They were domineering and manipulative, and did it all with a smile. If you were on their level at work, you were fine, but if you were a direct report or a threat, you were on their list, and not a list you wanted to be on.

One day at work, I was working on a high-profile project that my boss had ultimate responsibility for. It was the end of the day and I was off-site instead of working from my office. A situation arose that was out of my control, and as instructed, I called my boss to give the update. When I gave the update, out of nowhere, they started yelling at me. They were blaming me for something that I had no responsibility or accountability for. They continued yelling at me and degrading me on the phone in front of a colleague who was in their office. Ultimately, I was blamed for what happened, though it was completely out of my control. The stress in that moment was so intense that I got a spontaneous nose bleed. My fight or flight response was activated so intensely, that all rational thought left me. I was instantly filled with an ager and rage, with cortisol and adrenaline coursing through my body. I was ready for the fight of my life, even if it was only in my imagination. They hung up the phone on me after acting disgusted with me, and told me to figure it out, which I was eventually able to do and the fake crisis was averted. I closed things down for the day and headed back to my office. I threw my things down and slammed my office door. I was numb and angry, and the rational thinking part of my brain was eluding me.

In that moment, I wasn't my rational self. Something had changed in me. I pictured horrific things happening to my boss. I pictured dramatic, heroic stories of me putting them in their place and humiliating them like they had done to me. I pictured quitting without notice to "show them." I felt this intense uncomfortable energy coursing through my body. I couldn't be calmed and I was beside myself. I didn't know what was happening. In my mind, this person was a monster, and my ego couldn't let this go. It ate away at me for hours, while the disgust I had for this person lasted for months. I biked home and as soon as I walked into my apartment, I poured myself a stiff cocktail. A large glass of vodka on the rocks. By the time I was done with my second drink, the energy had subsided somewhat, but my hatred for them, for this event, and other events that involved working with them had reached a point of no return. While I stayed at this job for another two years after this, emotionally I quit that day. I was done.

Several months later, I realized what happened to me that day. The situation had caused such an emotional fight or flight response in me, triggering a response in me so intensely, that the part of my brain for logical thinking was shut off. I was in an amygdala hijack, and this wasn't the first time this had happened to me, but it was the most intense.

My simple explanation of amygdala hijack is that it is an exaggerated over-activation of our body's innate fight or flight safety response to a situation, whether or not it is actually a "life-threatening" situation. Amygdala hijack is a hyper-reactive out of proportion response to a situation that overrides the rational/thinking portion of the brain, called the prefrontal cortex. In a regular fight or flight response, the prefrontal cortex works alongside the amygdala, keeping rational thought at the forefront. In amygdala hijack, the prefrontal cortex is overridden and non-life-threatening situations, such as the stressful work situation I described, can lead to a response where we lose our rational thought processes and have this hijack response.

Like that day at work, so much of what we perceive in the world today elicits an intense stress hormone induced response that wreaks havoc on our bodies when it's stored and not released, or when we have the same persistent response to daily living. When we are in this hijack stress response mode, our rational, prefrontal cortex mind, which gives us rational thought and the ability to make decisions, is overridden.

Once I became aware of this, I knew when I was in hijack mode because I could feel it come over me. It felt like the world was coming down on me and I couldn't make a decision. I would catastrophize, making everything a life-or-death catastrophic event even when it wasn't, because the rational part of my mind, the prefrontal cortex, was no longer in the driver's seat. While this is helpful if you're being chased by a lion, it is not helpful when you are on a meeting with a manipulative boss or under so much stress at work or in personal life that you can't see a way out from under all of it. It's what I call a "short circuit" moment. My brain short-circuited and I couldn't see any way out when I was in hijack mode. It's an intense feeling of overwhelm or anxiety with a surge of strong emotions following it. Instead of thinking rationally, I was in a highly irrational reactive state based on intense emotional feelings.

When I would go into hijack mode, outside of alcohol, little would soothe or calm me as I didn't know what to do at the time. I had such intense emotional feelings towards a situation and I couldn't figure out what to do. And my pervasive, ruminating egoic thoughts were always along for the ride, convincing me I was the victim or martyr. I was so attached to these thoughts as I thought they defined me. In hindsight, once I knew what hijack was, I realized my rational thinking prefrontal cortex was overridden and I learned what to do.

But years ago, I didn't know what to do. I didn't want to have the alcoholic drink in order to escape, but it worked so quickly. It numbed and calmed me so nicely. I would feel the effect of the alcohol come over me and instantly knew I would be ok. At the time, I didn't know there were other action steps I could complete, but now I do. Knowledge is power, and the awareness I gained about amygdala hijack as well as sitting in acceptance and then performing next right action, such as a mindful breathing exercise or doing 50 jumping jacks, has helped immensely. Now I can intercept a hijack moment by utilizing the concepts in the paradigm and it's been such a game-changer.

While all of the actions on my life preserver list can help when in hijack mode, for me, many didn't work. They would lessen the hijack, but I would still feel uncomfortable in my skin and want to do something more to help get back into rational thinking. What worked for me most consistently was meditation, any intense workout, or my favorite for jolting me out of hijack, cold-water therapy, which I later found out was directly related to our mammalian dive reflex. For the cold-water therapy (and check with your health care provider to see if it's medically safe for you), I would take an ice-cold shower or at least put my head under cold water for as long as I could handle. Alternatively, I would dip my face or even my hands in a bucket of ice water for several seconds to shock my system out of hijack. It always worked in getting me out of hijack, and even if the feeling came back, the intensity of the feeling was much less.

While my goal is to not be in a situation where hijack even comes up, now I know how to name it and manage it. I know utilizing the paradigm along with daily meditation has helped me immensely. While I still react to certain stressful situations, any over-reactive response is lessening. My coping is better and I am more resilient; I have more adaptation energy. The stressful feeling dissolves quicker and doesn't leave scars like it used to. I don't store the stress in the same way as it's being released in the moment. I don't turn to alcohol or food for comfort. I turn to the paradigm and next right action. The most common action for me being meditation.

I am also aware that while the drinking helped in the immediate moment, it was simply a crutch. In order to break free from ongoing hijack of everyday living, and the lesser version of hijack that we call every day stress, I needed healthier coping mechanisms which would make me stronger and more resilient. The actions discussed in this chapter are from my arsenal. While I cannot control how someone treats me, I can control where I put my attention, if I even choose to give them my energy and attention, and how I respond to them. I choose my intention and then the next right action. By doing this, we begin to care for ourselves in a way where we can deal with a situation and let the stress go, instead of internalizing it and storing it for later.

Sending Love

Another action that has had a profound effect on me is the simple act of sending love to self and others. When I say others, it is also for individuals who you don't like—individuals who elicit an emotional response from you. In modern times, the amount of energy expended on people we don't like devours the energy we need for ourselves. When we send love, we are able to release the negative energy we have for someone and keep that priceless commodity of our energy for ourselves.

When I first heard it, I didn't like the concept of sending love to others who I don't like. Yes, I can send love to self and others, but why someone I don't like? What you attend to grows, and if you are filled with disdain or hatred for someone, it affects you more than them. Over time this changes you. That's why we send love. Like with forgiveness, sending love isn't about the other person as much as it is about me. I forgive to lift the burden I carry and set myself free, and I also send love to lift the burden and set myself free.

I learned that in sending love, we start with sending love to self, as many people struggle with self-love. Then we start by sending love to others. We often create enemies in our minds, along with vivid stories of how we are victimized by some other person. While it may be justified, this mental model does nothing to the other person. Like with holding a grudge, it only hurts us. What we want to do is to send love, in any way we can, no matter how small it may be, as it creates space for us to grow and keep our energy for ourselves.

Sometimes it's so hard to do, so try to think of this person as a helpless newborn or a cute toddler learning how to walk. At some point, all humans are cute and helpless. We picture our perceived nemesis as this cute helpless child and we send love. It may sound silly, but it's a way to change our reaction to a situation when we are faced with seeing that person. The energy it takes to send love is far less for us than the energy it takes to sustain and send disdain and hate.

Alternatively, there may be people and situations too horrific, that we can't even imagine sending love to them. That is fine. Send love to self as you release that negativity and surrender to something greater than you. Let go of the negative energy, the hate and disgust and anger you have. This is all about liberating you. Sending love has helped me release anger and hatred towards others in my life as my egoic thinking made them into horrific monsters. The energy I gave away was priceless and left me feeling empty and tired, resentful and angry. As I began letting go and forgiving, over time I was able to send love. And if I couldn't send love to them, I sent it to myself while letting go and moving on.

In my life, I created many scenarios of the villains in my life. My ego and I loved demonizing these "monsters" as my ego enjoyed playing the victim role. This is what the ego excels at, creating the biggest monster with the biggest stories about another person. When I started sending love, a shift happened in me. It wasn't the egoic monster that changed when I sent them love, but in fact it was I who changed. The needed change happened in me and the absolute dread I had around interacting with these "monsters" also decreased. Over time, I also realized they aren't monsters, but they are humans. It doesn't mean their actions aren't inappropriate or wrong, but it took the personal sting out of the situation. I would start to smile and laugh at the antics of people who my ego once perceived as enemies.

What I realized through this process is that I also bring energy to the table. This energy is palpable. Many of us have walked into a room and felt tension. We say to ourselves, "Something feels off." This energy can also be felt in one-on-one personal interactions. I noticed as I shifted and started sending love, I came to the table with a different presence. Suddenly, my perceived enemies didn't have any power over me anymore because I didn't give it to them. The energy I expended decreased exponentially as well. I was no longer depleted and exhausted by the end of the day because I kept my energy for me. I was able to come home, and instead of falling onto the couch, I'd be able to go for a bike ride or go to dinner with friends and not complain and story tell. It was truly liberating.

By sending love, I was healing my wounds and creating a better environment for me. This is what sending love is about. And when we are sending love to others, we always start with sending love to self first. Our self-love is the most important. Even if I don't feel it, on some level, we must uncover the truth that we are lovable, and that starts with sending love to self.

I have tried this technique on different people in my life whose personas would elicit an angry or an annoyed response. Anyone from celebrities and politicians I would see on TV as well as the everyday people in my life, some of which I initially wanted to avoid. As I continued sending love, I changed. I was less tense and more sincere. Challenging situations became less intense. There was a period of time where every day when I woke up, I felt a cloud over me. I couldn't shake it. I'd wake up, and with my eyes closed, I'd say to myself, "I send love, I send love, I send love. I send love to everyone I encounter. I send love to self, I send love to (insert name of challenging person), I send love. Love, love, love, love, love." This may sound silly, but it works.

The most challenging people I'd have to start with a compliment. One person I just couldn't send love to, but they wore nice socks, so I'd say, "Well, at least they have nice socks." It was a compliment of the least in nature that I could sincerely mean. I'd see them in the hall, and initially I'd have a grimace or negative thought. Then I'd mentally compliment their socks, or someone's eyeglass frames (yes, I did this with someone's glasses) to create this shift for me.

Prior to this, I tried to avoid so many situations because I didn't want these perceived enemies to be in my life. I had so many resentments of situations and people because I was so heavily attached to my ego and what it said about people who had wronged me. Once I started sending love to self and others, it became easier and easier for me. Eventually, I built up enough space and was keeping my energy for me. Now, it's almost automatic. I either picture them as that innocent cute toddler or compliment a necktie or item of clothing, and from there, create space to lessen egoic attachments to disliking, hating or demonizing people, to then sending love.

This has also created immense space in my life for self-compassion and compassion in others. We are all humans. We all have egos and egoic thoughts and attachments. Many of us are unaware of most of the concepts presented here in this book. Once we are able to start understanding the limitations we have had when we are attached to ego, we can have the same compassion and empathy for others when we see them clearly attached to their egos.

Sending love and giving compassion to others does not mean what they did or what they are doing is correct. It means that we see them as fallible and unaware that they are attached to their ego like we were. Now we can create that space needed to move from dislike, hate or disgust to empathy and ultimately to send love. This is where we begin, with ourselves. Once we do, we can then come to the table with compassion inside of us. Instead of trying to fight a daily war with someone, I came to the table to do what I needed to do. Though their actions may not change, it lessened the stress I felt and changed the energy I gave. Sending love helped me detach from association as one with my ego and what it said about people who "wronged" me, knowing in hindsight they hadn't at all. It was all just a story I was attached to as told to me by my ego. Sending love and utilizing the concepts of the paradigm helped me move from victim/martyr to empowered individual with a voice and a choice. This will happen for you as well when you send love. Go compliment someone's socks and see what happens!

Meditation

One action step that changed my life and I cannot overstate the effect of enough is meditation. Learning to meditate was one of the single greatest things I did as part of my wellness journey, as it ultimately led me out of the depths of depression and feelings of worthlessness, into a world of wellness, resiliency and self-love, while finding peace and fulfillment from within in this present moment. Though I have been practicing mindfulness techniques since the early 2000's, I learned a mantra-based meditation technique called Vedic meditation in 2015, and in 2024 I became a Vedic meditation teacher.

Meditation is one of the most profound experiences and exercises that helped change my life for the better. There are many types of meditation out there. I have taught guided meditation, mindfulness meditation, and now Vedic meditation. All of them are equally wonderful based on what you are trying to get out of it, and that is likely the ability to come back to present moment. Meditation is not about quieting the mind and Vedic meditation welcomes, yes welcomes, all of your many thoughts as part of the meditation, allowing you to transcend or go beyond thoughts, as you release stored stress. This allows you to build resilience or adaptation energy, and instead of constantly reacting to life, you start responding to life.

As we've discussed throughout this book, the mind and our thoughts are vibrantly alive and always on the go. For me, meditation helped me center myself, helping me to realize that I am separate from my thoughts as they are spinning and buzzing around in my head and gives me the necessary adaptation energy to get through the day. Without a meditation practice, we store and carry stress with us inside our bodies. Small things add up over time and this often manifests in the body as physical and psychological ailments, like insomnia, headaches, muscle tension and pain, weight fluctuations, skin problems, digestive issues or teeth grinding just to name a few.

Guided meditation helped me let go and calm my nervous system. Mindfulness meditation brought me back to the beauty of present moment and Vedic meditation combined the two, giving me the long-term benefits of resiliency due to the ongoing adaptation energy I received through a twice daily mantra-based meditation practice. I feel things more deeply and more fully and more intensely. I am able to let go of past emotional attachments differently and embrace the beauty of today. It doesn't mean I don't have bad days, and it's no magic pill, but it is something I cannot imagine my life without.

Without awareness, many of us turn life's every day events into stressors that we end up storing in our bodies. This stress adds up over time and when something happens and we get angry, rarely are we solely angry at the situation in front of us. While it may partially be anger with the current situation, there is more stored emotional energy behind it waiting to be released because of not dealing with our feelings and emotions like we discussed in Chapter 10 with Lean In & Let Go. The same can be said with sorrow and fear. These emotions are stored in our bodies, whether we knowingly suppressed them or unknowingly repressed them. When we don't realize it, they manifest from other situations and can be overwhelming because we haven't dealt with them. The stress release through meditation helps us release these trapped emotions. As we grow in our meditation practice, we experience the same situations differently and stop storing stressful events. We still experience them fully, but not with the detrimental physical and psychological effects we once did. We no longer suppress and repress events in our lives. We feel them as they are happening. This change occurs over time if we can just get over the hump and start meditating.

In meditation, there is a term that is used called "unstressing." Unstressing occurs during and after meditation. It is the release of stress and tension that has been built up and carried by the body for years. Carrying this stress has many effects on the human psyche and our physical bodies. Quite often, we aren't even aware that we are carrying this stress, which as we discussed, often manifests as headaches, muscle tension, and so on. We meditate in order to release these stored stresses, allowing us to live life more fully. The benefit of regular meditation is that we no longer store new stresses. We have the experiences, but are no longer repressing or suppressing.

One day in meditation teacher training, we were given an analogy about meditators vs. non-meditators as follows: Non-meditators have experiences that are chiseled in stone, meaning they store the negative energy. Infrequent meditators or new meditators have the experiences forged in sand. A gentle breeze comes by and smooths the sand over, no longer storing it. Experienced meditators have experiences just as fully as the first two scenarios, but now the chisel cuts through water, no longer leaves a mark in the water. This is how meditation builds resiliency—we have the same experiences, but we process them differently. This is our adaptation energy growing, and the more adaptation energy we have, the better coping skills we have to navigate daily life.

When we begin to meditate, we immediately start releasing our fight or flight stress hormones (e.g. cortisol and adrenaline) which wreak havoc on our bodies. We aren't meant to be in a constant state of fight or flight, but in our modern world, we are. This leads to fatigue, heart disease, digestive problems, insomnia, depression, anxiety, and weight gain as a few examples. When we meditate, we are able to release the stresses of everyday life and gain that precious adaptation energy which gives us resiliency. Life still happens, but now we are interacting with it differently. We feel it more fully, finding contentment and happiness from within, allowing us to embrace the "is-ness" of life. We start to engage our parasympathetic nervous system which some call the "rest, digest and heal" nervous system. It is in this state that our bodies literally rest, digest our food and start to heal. Without this, adrenaline and cortisol from our fight or flight response continue to cause physical and mental illnesses that affect our daily lives and we don't even question it anymore.

There are so many benefits of twice daily Vedic meditation, and if you can't do twice daily, start with 5 min every morning before getting out of bed. Twice daily may seem like a lot, but when the benefits are so clear and knowing that thoughts were a welcome part of this practice, it was easy for me to find the time and make it a part of my daily routine. And most importantly, the return on investment for your time is tenfold. It gave me my life back and is so worth it. Regardless of the type of meditation that interests you, start today. Visit ImperfectionWellness.com for more information on learning how to meditate.

Mindful Breathing

One of my favorite next right actions is a breathing technique called mindful Breathing. Mindful breathing is so simple. We will do it now. As you are reading this, bring your awareness to your breath. As you continue reading, pay subtle attention to the inhale, then to the exhale. Continue paying subtle attention to your breathing as you read the rest of this chapter. Find a way to bring mindful breathing into your daily life, if even for a moment, such as when reading a book, brushing your teeth or washing your hands. When you bring mindful breathing into everyday living, you are creating mental space by momentarily disconnecting from egoic thoughts and reconnecting with present moment. The more you do this on a daily basis, the easier it will be to detach from pervasive, ruminating thoughts.

When you utilize this breathing technique, you bring your awareness to two places, to your breathing, and to the action at hand, thus allowing you to stay in present moment. Again, as you continue reading the rest of this chapter, pay attention to the subtle inhale and exhale as you read, knowing you will forget. When you realize you've forgotten, simply and effortlessly come back to the technique, if only for a moment.

At first it may feel uncomfortable, but over time, it becomes easier. When you practice this in the calm state, it is easier to do in a stressful state as you are strengthening a new muscle. When you do this in a stress-induced state, you are better able to cope with the situation at hand, staying in present moment, instead of going into an unnecessary stress response. This breathing technique allows you to cope better with life, and helps keep the rational thinking, pre-frontal cortex area of your brain engaged.

Setting Boundaries

Setting boundaries as a next right action is about protecting yourself and your time, so you can be at your best. Ask yourself, "Do I need to set any boundaries?" The answer is likely yes. And if so, you can set boundaries by starting with simple requests, saying something as simple as, "No, I'm not able to do that" or "Sorry, that won't work for me." With this step and the entire process of the paradigm, we start realizing what we want to do to support our wellbeing. Yes, there will be compromises with certain people in our lives, but that doesn't mean I need to take care of *you*, whoever *you* are. Many times, all that we do in hopes of trying to please others leaves us feeling exhausted, small, and sometimes resentful of that person. Through this process, we can start to set boundaries, and in taking care of ourselves first, we are then better able to be there for those who we want to share our time with.

Additionally, "No," is a complete sentence. "I am not able to do that," or "That isn't going to work out for me," are two other statements I use. As a former people pleaser, I always said yes and put myself second, then resented the other person for my response of saying yes to something I didn't want to do. Now that I am aware and have let go of putting other's needs before mine, I prioritize my needs and wants, compromising when appropriate with certain individuals who mean the most to me. And when I do not want to or cannot do something, "No," or "I'm not able to," is my go-to statement. No emotional energy, no worry or ruminating thoughts. Just a simple, no.

How many times do we say yes, to please someone so we don't hurt their feelings, only to end up doing something we don't want to do or don't have time to do. Then we resent the other person for *our* decision and cause stress to ourselves. If we were honest with ourselves from the start, respecting ourselves and the other person, a simple no would have prevented all of this. Try it today. Start with something simple and have your boundary statement ready.

The Life Preserver List

My life preserver list is a list of action items to have on the ready for the times when my ego would creep up on me and catch me off guard. As my fried Missy says, "When someone is drowning, you don't teach them how to swim. You throw them a life preserver and rescue them." That is how I thought about my list. This list of actions was my life preserver. We don't create the action list when we are overwhelmed. We create this list when we have a better perspective of things. The list is made up of personalized actions that we can reference when these feelings of overwhelm come over us.

I sometimes take a quick look at my list before heading out to a social function that may lead to me feeling social anxiety, and I become grounded in self and present moment. I go into the situation prepared and ready. This is especially helpful for the times when others are drinking and I am not, since drinking was my social lubricant for so many years. I would often go into a panic mode before certain social situations. I wouldn't know what to do so I'd drink to relax. Now, instead of drinking, I will go to my list. One of the intentions and action items on my list was to go into the party and enjoy everyone's company (intention) and the action was to repeat a simple mantra to myself, "I surrender this fear and worry, knowing I got this. I am going to be ok." I would say that over and over to myself, flooding myself with positive thoughts while sending myself love at the same time. This is just one example of how I use my life-preserver list.

I created this action plan list to easily reference when I was overwhelmed or frozen on the couch so I could get out of association with my thoughts and back to present moment. I needed something I could look at to help me when I knew I couldn't think of ideas for activities to get me unstuck. I needed something to reference, so I could choose one or more actions to get me back to present moment.

By doing one or more of these actions on my life preserver list, I was able to feel that I am separate from my thoughts and break the immediate cycle through next right action. It was liberating and began my healing and recovery to begin loving myself. When I am in association with my thoughts and can't find a way out; and/or it's too uncomfortable to "Lean In & Let Go", I have a list of actions ready to help support my intentions and I share them here with you. These actions are nothing fancy, but they brought me back into rational thought processes which allowed me to come back into present moment living, ultimately finding my happiness from within.

The list below is far from complete, but everything listed below is on my current life preserver list. Each person will have something different that works for them. My old list had "play guitar" and "exercise" on it. But when I was down and out, those were too hard for me. So, if you're anything like me, you need simple and achievable action steps that jump start you from a phase one action like washing your hands to a phase two action like learning to play guitar.

When you are in a state of mind where you can't think of something to do, you can reference this list. The goal here is to be aware you are redirecting your thinking to get into an action and gain the physical and mental momentum of moving forward.

These activities are not meant for you to escape from what is going on, but instead, get you back to present moment living, getting you out of association with a pervasive, ruminating thought cycle that leads to inaction. We don't want to create mindless distractions that allow us to go back into repression or suppression of our thoughts and emotions, but to create actions that keep you moving forward, aligned with an intention.

Before we go into action, we bring awareness that we are doing this action consciously to create some space from the feeling, emotion or emotional event leading to the overwhelming feelings. This gives us a cooling off period. Once we have had some time and space from the emotion, we come back in order to lean in and let go so it is fully addressed and will no longer be stored as a repressed or suppressed event.

The Life Preserver List

Below is a sample from my actual Life Preserver List and free examples of the first three bullet points can be found on ImperfectionWellness.com.

- Meditate or listen to a guided meditation.

- Listen to a podcast on wellness.

- Use mala beads and recite a universal mantra like Om Mani Padme Hum or On Namo Guru Dev Namo

- Focus on your breath, e.g. perform Mindful Breathing

- Read a book.

- Take a free online lesson to teach yourself how to play guitar.

- Cook or bake and take it into your coworkers.

- Volunteer to get groceries for a neighbor or friend.

- Do simple cleaning, e.g. wipe the counter down with a damp cloth, just start somewhere and break the large overwhelming task into simple action steps that you can achieve.

- Listen to music.

- Walk or run outside.

- Go to the park.

- Watch funny blooper reels online.

- Go for bike ride.

- Go online and teach yourself how to make a paper airplane or origami art.

- Write an affirmation and list one thing you are grateful for.

- Play with a dog or pet or ask a neighbor if you can walk their dog.

- Make a list of 5 tasks that are so simple (e.g. throwing a wrapper away) then do one or more of the tasks and check the box as completed for a feeling of accomplishment.

- Put guardrails around your social media scrolling, in the content you view, who you follow and how long you allow yourself to be on social media. Ask yourself, "Am I trying to escape or numb? What is another next right action?" Never judge yourself if you fall into a social media rabbit hole. Simply forgive yourself and move on, trying to do better next time. You are human, so embrace your humanness.

- Do any task or activity at half speed, bringing you back to present moment.

Setting an Intention and Performing Next Right Action:

Set an intention to get unstuck from your thoughts as you come back to present moment living, finding inner-happiness and fulfillment from within.

Set an intention to meditate. If you don't know how, visit ImperfectionWel lness.com to learn a simple meditation technique. A note on meditation: It's not about sitting with your legs crossed and your fingers pointed upwards, as your hands rest on your legs. Sure, you can do that, but meditation is so much more. And the meditation I teach is about allowing your thoughts instead of trying to stop them. So, to me, as a biased meditation teacher, meditation is for everyone since we all have thousands of thoughts a day!

Set an intention to breathe! Quite often in today's daily living, we don't take deep breaths anymore. There are numerous studies you can find outlining the benefits of breathing. Several of my favorite breathing exercises are below:

- **Pranayama Alternate Nostril Breathing and Left Nostril Breathing**

- **Box Breathing**

- **Mantra breathing with the universal mantra, *So Hum***

- **Visit ImperfectionWellness.com to learn these techniques**

Set an intention to send love. Start with love of self, then send love to the perceived "bad person". Can't send them love? Send love to their two-year-old self. Still can't send love, then send love to self again and be proud you tried.

Set an intention to let go, to forgive, and to surrender.

Set an intention to accept what is, exactly as it is and was, knowing our lives are the sum total of our choices up to this present moment.

Set an intention to relinquish attachments, to be the observer, and to embrace the amazingly wonderful empowered person you are.

Set the intention to align with True Self as you say the following affirmation, "I am Beautiful! I am Strong! I am Worth It! I am Enough!" Set an intention of gratitude.

Set an intention to move! Just get up and move! Walk around your apartment or house. Just open the front door and walk around the block (this was hard for me when I was at my worst but now is an easy favorite). Go outside even if you come right back in. Any physical activity shifts your brain from thinking to an action and this works. Alternatively, do 25 to 50 jumping jacks; Or just jump up and down for 30 seconds. Try it—it works!

When in amygdala hijack, and if medically safe for you, take an ice-cold shower, put your face or even your hands in a container of cold ice water, or wash your hands with the coldest tap water you can. There are studies saying this gives you a dopamine boost (the feel-good hormone) that lasts for several hours after and can get you out of amygdala hijack. Not fond on taking a cold shower? Do 25 jumping jacks. The goal here is to break the hijack cycle!

Set an intention to mentally pull back and expand your view of a situation. When you are in a situation, you are on top of it. Mentally pull back to several feet away. Expand your perspective. Pull back to 100 feet. Then pull back to 5,000 feet, then 30,000 feet and see the entire view by expanding your sample size. How does that problem feel from the view of the 30,000 feet vs right in front of your face? Looking at a problem from this lens would help me get unstuck.

Alternatively, you can try the *Rule of Fives*: How will you feel five hours from now? Five days from now? Five weeks from now? Five months from now? Five years from now? Asking yourself how you will feel with the Rule of Fives give you automatic perspective that this feeling or its current intensity won't last forever.

Set an intention for self-calming. Gently tap on your sternum (the middle of your chest right above your nipple line) for 1-2 minutes as you practice mindful breathing. This helps activate the vagus nerve and the parasympathetic (rest, digest and heal) nervous system.

Set an intention to be active. Any physical activity that can redirect your brain to positivity that is easy to accomplish. There is nothing wrong with saying "I will do a 30-minute workout when I am stuck." But when I was stuck, the idea of a 30-minute workout overwhelmed me. Then I felt like a failure and the cycle continued. Instead, I would walk outside or do 25 jumping jacks. These physical activities were easily accomplished and then I continued simple actions from my list until it broke the pattern of association. 25 jumping jacks is great because two things are going on. You are physically moving and counting. By default, you come back to the present moment because you can't be associated with your thoughts while jumping and counting.

Knit, crochet or needlepoint. It's right there in your lap. And as you do it, keep a simple mantra going like, "I am beautiful, I am strong, I am worth it, I am enough!"

Laugh. Laugh a lot. Laugh hard. Go online and watch a blooper's reel from your favorite TV show or a baby laughing. Stay away from toxic news stories and graphic movies that can overwhelm you and your nervous system.

Cook or bake. Focusing on a recipe gets my mind somewhere else. And I enjoy searching for healthy recipes to try at home. My favorite was when I was watching a TV baking competition and was inspired to create an 8-strand plaited loaf of bread. It was amazing and got my mind of my thoughts for a while!

Call someone, anyone. Call a friend! They aren't there? Call another friend. Still no answer, try scheduling a call with a close friend. "Hey, can you call me by end of day? Just need to chat for a bit."

What else can you commit to that is simple and easy? Make a list and make the action steps doable for you!

Lastly, though the paradigm was life saving for me, and this 'action' section was paramount to me getting out of association with my thoughts, feelings and emotions, I am here to say that it still happens rather frequently, that out of nowhere when I least expect it, I am back in association with my thoughts and sometimes don't realize it until a spiral has begun.

And still, with all the work I have done, I don't always recognize when I am in association with my thoughts right away. I've had sleepless anxiety ridden nights and that is usually when I realize, "Oh NO! I am back associated as one with my thoughts! 911 emergency!" Then I come back to the section of the paradigm needed to help me, and many times it is this action section.

I can't underscore enough the importance of this section. And, because you are a beautiful human who was associated with thoughts and ego most of your life, you will have moments where you re-associate with these thoughts and that is ok. Because now, you have an amazing arsenal in your toolbox with this paradigm to get you back to present moment.

The difference now is that I recognize it sooner, and every action listed I've tried and I know what works better for me and what to use in combination of several of the actions for those challenging moments. The reason I share this is that when I found a reprieve from my thoughts, I thought I was fixed, cured, and unbroken. But a day or two later something would 'set me off' and I'd go right back to association with my thoughts, and feel lost and overwhelmed again.

What I realized, is that the ego is a part of us and always will be. I don't fight the ego, but I don't always realize it's come back out to try and take me down, so that is why I say I live the paradigm every day of my life. It's easy now because it's just a part of me. Ten universal truths arranged into nine pillars leading me to present moment awareness, as True Self, finding my contentment from within, and this is also my wish for you!

14

Finding Your True Self

When we learn these universal truths, and apply the concepts of Possley's Paradigm, we begin to unwind the tangled web of the ego, and it's control and influence over our lives. The gains we make will be profound, but there will be moments where we think to ourselves that it's not working. Be aware of this, as it may be the ego creeping back in, bringing back more fear, leading you to want to escape or numb or avoid or suppress or repress again. Hold fast to your newfound knowledge, and continue applying the concepts, each and every day. Instead of thinking of it as additional work, think of it as working towards a path to liberation and investing in yourself. Keep coming back to the paradigm, keep learning more about these universal truths, and keep applying the concept that you learn here.

Contentment and fulfillment from within do not mean a life of perfection. It's ups and downs with sorrows, trials and tribulations that build character and give us resiliency so we can live life more fully and embrace all that life has to offer, its joys and its sorrows, which are a guarantee. It's not a hall pass to a perfect happy life. There is no such thing. That is an illusion. To be human is to be imperfect; to fall and get up again, to fall once more and still get up. It's this resiliency that we are trying to achieve, not a hedonistic life of perfect happiness all the time. We will suffer losses but will be able to look at them as learning opportunities and a part of life instead of being victimized by them. We are now empowered to live more fully in the present moment, knowing, "Even though this hurts, this too shall pass and I will be ok!"

The goal of the paradigm is to help people find and enjoy their authentic True Self, while coming back to present moment living. We now know that we are not our thoughts and what they say about us and the world around us. We have them, but we are separate from them. It helps us navigate the ups and downs of the world we live in, taking present moment as it is. It helps us not live with regret of the past or fears of the future. It helps us identify when the ego is in story-telling mode, rating, comparing and judging myself and others. This is true liberation, allowing us to live our lives more fully!

Over time, we start to build resilience and gain adaptation energy, which allows us to be able to cope better with life situations. The paradigm isn't a bulletproof vest that prevents us from feeling, or makes everything idyllic and fine. Quite the opposite occurs. We will often feel things more intensely, but we don't store the negative energy inside us. We still have bad days and stressful moments, but now we have a way to cope with them.

In its entirety, the paradigm is an action plan to help you become more than what your thoughts say about you, while living with contentment and fulfillment in the present moment. We learn to accept life as it is, was and will be. And we learn to separate from the ever-needy ego and its never-ending commentary about everything around you. We start to associate more as our True Self, no longer interested in judging, rating and comparing ourselves and others.

The ten concepts are the launching points for me. When I am in egoic thinking and out of present moment living, living as small self instead of True Self, I now have a reference tool to help me get out of egoic thinking patterns and come back to present moment reality. That is also why I created the daily journal and have included it in this book. The ten concepts are weaved into the journal questions to reinforce what we are learning. This helps us so that the ideas become second nature to us. It is nice that we learned about them, but now we are able to live them by utilizing the included daily journal. There were times when I have used the journal and barely got through the questions because I was not feeling the vibe whatsoever. Then several hours later, I noticed a lighter feeling. It was directly related to my using the journal, which helped me to recenter on present moment.

I also don't want people to think that this is a "one and done, read it and things will instantly be better" type of book. Instead, it is an introduction to the concepts of True Self, Egoic Thinking and Present Moment Living. When we understand these concepts and have tools to get unstuck from patterned egoic thinking, we begin to find contentment and fulfillment from within. We begin to enjoy the world around us instead of feeling small, victimized, resentful, stressed and lost, simply going through the motions. It is such a part of my daily life that it doesn't feel like additional work. It is just how I live now.

I still have bad days, but because my foundation is strong and centered, my recovery is quicker with less scars and battle wounds. I still have sad moments and I still get anxious or overwhelmed at times, but now I have a blueprint, a roadmap to address the fear-based emotions and move forward with agility. I have moments of anger and they pass more easily. All my emotions still come and go. I am not fighting with or trying to suppress my emotions anymore. This paradigm isn't a preventative insurance policy that says everything will be perfect. It isn't protective bubble wrap or insulation from life. Instead, it is designed to help us deal with what life has to offer. And life offers everything, from happiness, to sadness, to joy and to tragedy, and everything in between. We will feel our emotions and have our responses to life, but now we will not be caste down in shackles, suffering indefinitely from what life offers.

I have a family member with a health diagnosis that is hard to watch, knowing there is no cure. While I am saddened to see this, I do not sink to the depths of despair and depression like I would have in the past. Some of our interactions are wonderful and I feel those moments more fully. Due to the waxing and waning nature of the disease, some of our interactions are painful and sad. I know that "this too shall pass," as all things in life do. I have a stronger foundation to build on and I stay in present moment instead of story-telling about what the future holds, knowing sometimes I'm going to cry and others times laugh like there's no tomorrow. It's hard and I grieve for what's happening but I'm not lost in it like I would have been years ago. The concepts of the paradigm support my mental health and wellness and it's far better than the alternative of depression, anxiety, fear, regret, and drinking to escape, suppress, repress, and numb.

The steps of the paradigm do not try to change the picture of my past into a pretty picture, if in fact it were a bad one. Terrorizing moments from my past were still terrorizing in that moment from years prior, but now my attachment and my emotional association with it has changed. I have let go of the story-telling and attachment with those moments. After much time (many years in some cases), I leaned into acceptance of what happened, and appreciate the experiences for what I learned and how I have grown since those moments

Some moments in life are so troubling, that I would never suggest we move on from them immediately. Our brain and bodies are still processing what just occurred or recently occurred. Time gives us the perspective to pull up from the ground, moving from a few feet away, giving us that needed 30,000-foot view. It may take an hour, or a year, or many years to get the perspective that time gives us, and that's ok.

Life isn't a sprint and there is no rush to get to the end. The only end we have comes in the form of present moment. There are experiences in my life from a few months ago that I am still working through. I give myself the needed compassion, free of any judgment or comparison, and let myself heal, while using the concepts in the paradigm. Situations from five, ten or twenty years ago no longer have the same sting. And since I have viewed these stories with a new lens, and faced them head on for what they were, most of these events no longer haunt me or hurt me in the same way they did when they occurred.

This is the evolution of self that we see when we apply these principles. This is why I think this work is so import. I never had a playbook or reference guide. I thought it was just me and that I was broken. In working on this book and Imperfection Wellness, I have come to realize many people suffer in silence, or watch a loved one suffer in silence. Now that we have a play book, we can utilize these ten universal truths and you can modify them to work for you.

From a source of True Self, you are born *PERFECTLY* Imperfect and we are all on this journey together, always remembering that *I am more than what my thoughts say about me*! So, let's be nicer to ourselves and each other, as there is more about us that unites us than divides us!

Using the Paradigm

I'm often asked, "How can I apply the paradigm to my life?" To me, the answer is simple—I apply it to every aspect of my life.

I used to be an over-thinker, and I've struggled with ruminating thoughts, but now, I interact differently with my thoughts and self-beliefs. This paradigm has been a game changer for me because I use it daily. At first, this might seem like extra work, but as you begin to implement it, you realize you're getting your life back. You're learning to live more authentically and you can't put a price on that. It's worth the investment.

You start to interact with your false beliefs about yourself and engage with your thoughts in a new way. They no longer control you. Instead, you live with greater authenticity, fulfillment, and a deep sense of contentment and self-worth from within.

With that in mind, here's a list of **real-world situations** where the paradigm can help:

Letting go of anger – Releasing resentment and recognizing that holding onto anger only prolongs your suffering.

Accepting where you are in life as the sum total of choices – Shifting from regret to empowerment by embracing past decisions as part of personal growth.

Breaking free from the need for constant busyness – Recognizing that nonstop activity is often a form of avoidance while learning to be present.

Releasing attachment to external validation – Letting go of the need for approval from others to find your self-worth, instead, finding your self-worth from within.

Overcoming imposter syndrome – Recognizing self-doubt as a thought pattern, not a reflection of reality, and stepping into confidence.

Letting go of the need to be right – Choosing peace over ego-driven arguments and learning to accept differing perspectives.

Finding fulfillment beyond material possessions and societal status – Detaching self-worth from achievements and external markers of success.

Shifting from people-pleasing to authentic self-expression – Learning to say no, set boundaries, and prioritize personal needs without guilt.

Breaking free from perfectionism – Accepting mistakes and imperfections as part of growth rather than a source of shame.

Recognizing when the ego is seeking drama or conflict – Becoming aware of patterns that create unnecessary stress or chaos and choosing a different response.

Detaching from old, false identity labels – Releasing past definitions of self that no longer serve personal growth.

Navigating loneliness without seeking external distractions – Learning to sit with solitude and find contentment within.

Moving from resistance to acceptance in difficult life situations – Letting go of control and embracing what is, rather than what should be.

Releasing the grip of guilt and shame – Understanding that past mistakes do not define self-worth while choosing self-compassion.

Breaking the habit of negative self-talk – Shifting internal dialogue to be more supportive and kind.

Trusting intuition over fear-based decision-making – Learning to follow inner nudges instead of overanalyzing every choice.

Shifting from hyper-productivity to present-moment awareness – Finding balance between ambition and the ability to be fully present.

Recognizing the ego's comparison trap – Letting go of self-judgment based on how others appear to be doing.

Breaking cycles of avoidance and facing discomfort with awareness – Addressing difficult emotions rather than numbing or distracting from them.

Healing from past relationships without attaching to the story of hurt – Moving forward without allowing past wounds to shape self-identity.

Detaching from the belief that happiness comes from the next achievement – Realizing that fulfillment is found in the present, not in future accomplishments.

Recognizing the difference between true needs and ego-driven wants – Understanding what genuinely supports well-being versus what is an illusion of fulfillment.

Understanding that emotions are temporary and not self-defining – Observing emotions without attaching identity to them.

Seeking support to stop using drinking, sex, drugs, shopping, exercise or other actions as a numbing or coping behavior – Breaking free from dependence on numbing behaviors and finding clarity, peace, and self-trust in the sometimes uncomfortable present moment.

Calming the chaos and sitting with self and thoughts – Learning to embrace stillness instead of seeking constant distraction.

Stopping mindless scrolling – Becoming aware of unconscious habits and reclaiming time and attention.

Stopping ruminating thoughts – Recognizing repetitive negative thinking and shifting to a more present-focused mindset.

Lessening anxiety – Realizing you are separate from anxious thoughts and cultivating inner calm.

Changing the stories we tell ourselves about others and ourselves – Reframing limiting beliefs and shifting perspectives to foster growth.

Addressing self-doubt – Recognizing insecurity as a thought pattern, not a truth, and stepping into confidence.

Letting go – Releasing attachments to control, expectations, and past experiences, realizing that *insistence equals resistance.*

Surrendering and lessening control – Accepting what is and finding peace in the unknown.

Most importantly, *__learning to love yourself__* – Becoming aware that you are more than what your thoughts say about you and the world around you, accepting who you are, what you are, and where you are, while sitting in the discomfort, knowing this too shall pass. As you surrender, forgive yourself and others, and stop letting attachments define your self-worth. Become the observer of your thoughts and beliefs, letting go of stored emotions and false stories. Find an affirmation that works for you, ground yourself in gratitude, set an intention, and perform the next right action.

When we separate ourselves from the stories our egoic thoughts create, we step into the vastness of who we truly are as we uncover the boundless power within us. The true essence of our True Self lies in the awareness that we are not our thoughts, feelings or emotions, though we do have them. With this awareness, the world becomes limitless, and our potential unfolds in infinite ways. This understanding propels us forward, where the sky is no longer the limit. It is the endless horizon of who we are meant to be—and capable of becoming!

Scott W Possley

Your journey doesn't end here—it's just beginning!

True transformation happens when knowledge turns into action, and I want to help you take that next step. That's why I've created a **free 28-day journal** designed to guide you in applying these powerful concepts to your daily life. Through intentional reflection, thought-provoking prompts, and simple yet profound exercises, this journal will help you deepen your awareness, break free from limiting thought patterns, and cultivate lasting inner peace in less than 10 minutes a day.

Download it now at ImperfectionWellness.com/Journal and commit to your wellness journey—because the most meaningful changes happen one mindful day at a time and *you are worth the investment*!

15

Summary: Ten Universal Truths

Awareness: I am aware that I have thousands of thoughts each day and this is normal. I am aware that I am more than what these thoughts say about me and the world around me. I am aware that I am separate from these thoughts and that they are not based in truth. They are fragments, half-truths and stories from the past and future. I am aware that when I am identified as one with the thoughts, I am out of present moment living and it is unlikely that I feel happy or fulfilled as our egoic thoughts always want more.

Attachment: Ego creates attachment to people, places, things, ideas, opinions, thoughts, and self-beliefs. When attached, I can become paralyzed at the thought of not having them because my self-worth becomes tied to these attachments. I become aware that I am more than my egoic attachments. Releasing our egoic attachments doesn't mean I can't enjoy these items, ideas, and opinions. It simply means I am not defined by them. I know I am more than my attachments. I can relinquish, surrender and let go of the emotional attachments I have.

Acceptance: I fully accept everything in my life exactly as it is, the good and the bad, knowing that the past is over, and the future is an unknown. I accept that I am the sum total of all of my choices, and I know I always have a choice, as tough as that choice may be. I sit in present moment, fully accepting everything exactly as it currently is, was, or will be. I know I am where I am because of my choices, and my choices today influence tomorrow. And I am aware that there are other variables outside of my control influencing my tomorrow, and that sitting in acceptance doesn't mean I don't work towards goals for tomorrow.

Be the Observer (of our thoughts and self-beliefs): I have thoughts like everyone else. As I am separate from my thoughts, I choose to be the observer. My thoughts are separate from me and go by like I am watching a movie, a parade or as passing clouds in the sky. I am the observer of all my thoughts as they go by, saying to myself, "I am separate from my thoughts. I am more than what my thoughts say about me and the world around me."

Surrender: When a situation, thought or idea is too much for me to handle, I put my hands out and surrender to something outside of and greater than me: God, Nature, The Universe, Consciousness, etc. I drop the oars and become the water. I surrender control knowing "this" is bigger than me & will work itself out. Surrender doesn't mean I don't care—it means I trust that the answer is already there or will reveal itself in time once I let go of trying to control every variable. It acknowledges that I may not currently see the solution, but by releasing my grip, I create space for clarity, growth, and guidance to emerge naturally.

Lean-in & Let Go: When I feel an uncomfortable thought, feeling, or emotion come over me, I sit and get centered with my feet firmly planted on the ground instead of pushing it back down. I lean in and feel what is coming up and take slow deep breaths for 3-5 minutes as the energy around this sensation is released and slowly dissolves. The goal is to breathe through the sensation, refraining from numbing, avoiding, distracting, repressing, or suppressing the feeling or emotion. I let it come up and sit in the discomfort. I let go of the judgments, ratings, and comparisons of the ego. I let go of attachment with the thought, I let go of association with the thought. I let go of the idea that the thought defines me. I let go each and every time the thought comes up that tells me I am less than or better than someone else.

Forgiveness: When I forgive, it doesn't mean what happened wasn't wrong or make what happened ok. I forgive for me, if and when I want to, on my terms, when I am ready to, so I can heal and be free of the emotional burden I am carrying. I don't have to forget, and I likely won't, but I forgive and move on for my sake, on my timeline. Forgiveness is about me and also about lessening my emotional connection with a situation that is no longer serving my greater good. It's an individualized personal decision and I am the only one who can decide if and when I am ready to forgive. And if I can't forgive, I show myself self-compassion and let myself off the hook as forgiveness is a journey.

Affirmations & Gratitude: Move into an abundance mindset with affirmations & gratitude. Affirmations & Gratitude are written and said daily to reframe our thinking and shift our mindset from lack and scarcity to one of plenty and abundance. The paradigm affirmation is, "I am beautiful. I am strong. I am worth it. I am enough!" And if you aren't sure what to be grateful for, be grateful for your senses, that you can smell a flower or taste your favorite meal, hear your favorite song or read your favorite book. While you are always encouraged to feel what you are feeling at any given moment, knowing "this too shall pass," Affirmations & Gratitude help take the edge off of a bad day so you don't go into a negative spiral.

Action: When you are associated with thought and are stuck emotionally, or physically can't get off the couch, set a clear intention and act mindfully. Meditate, do 25 jumping jacks, go for a walk, mindfully wash your hands, any of which can cause an action chain reaction! Get unstuck from ruminating thoughts and overwhelming feelings or emotions by performing next right action. In such anxious or depressed states, one can feel physically and emotionally locked down. Take action, any action! Launch into an activity for you which creates space and separation from your egoic ruminating thoughts!

Visit ImperfectionWellness.com to learn more about Possley's Paradigm.

Additional Resources for Your Wellness Journey

Additional Resources for Your Wellness Journey

Always know that asking for help is a sign of strength! Taking the first step to seek support is not a sign of weakness, but a courageous act of self-love. No matter where you are on your journey, these resources are here to support, guide, and empower you. This list is in no way exhaustive, but a list of resources I have used myself over the years and I share them with you, knowing there are many more out there available to you.

Imperfection Wellness
Visit **ImperfectionWellness.com** for tools, insights, and practices to help you integrate Possley's Paradigm into your daily life. Explore articles, guided meditations, and resources designed to deepen your connection with the True Self and find lasting inner peace.

NAMI (National Alliance on Mental Illness) Hotline/Textline
If you or someone you know needs support, the **NAMI Helpline** is available at **800-950-NAMI (6264)** or via text by sending **"HELPLINE" to 62640.** This resource offers free, confidential support and information on mental health conditions, treatment options, and more.

988: The National Crisis & Suicide Prevention Hotline
Dial **988** anytime, anywhere for immediate support from trained crisis counselors. Whether you're struggling with thoughts of ending your life, emotional distress, or substance use, this lifeline is available 24/7 to provide compassionate assistance.

Psychology Today – Find a Therapist
Finding the right therapist can transform your wellness journey. Visit **Psychology Today** to search for qualified mental health professionals in your area or online, tailored to your needs and preferences.

ZocDoc – Find a Therapist
ZocDoc.com makes it easy to book therapy appointments. Visit to connect with therapists covered by your insurance or offering virtual sessions that fit your schedule.

Why These Resources Matter

Life's challenges are meant to be shared, not faced alone. Reaching out for help when you're feeling overwhelmed, stuck, or in pain is one of the most empowering steps you can take. These resources provide vital support systems, offering professional guidance, community, and hope. Remember, asking for help is not only a sign of strength but a profound act of self-care. Let these resources guide you as you embrace a more fulfilling and balanced life. **You are not alone. You matter and you are worth it!**

Note: I have no affiliation or personal interest in any of the resources listed here aside from Imperfection Wellness. These are just a few of the many resources available to support your wellness journey. I encourage you to conduct your own search to explore additional free or low-cost options that. may suit your needs.

About the author

About the author

S cott W. Possley is the founder of Imperfection Wellness, Wellness for the *PERFECTLY* Imperfect! He is a wellness visionary dedicated to helping others uncover their inner strength and live more authentically. With over 20 years experience as a physician assistant in some of New York City's top academic medical centers, Scott has combined his extensive medical expertise with a deep passion for mental health and holistic wellness. As a Vedic Meditation teacher, he merges evidence-based practices with ancient wisdom to offer a unique, transformative approach to personal growth.

His work is anchored in the principles of **Possley's Paradigm**, a framework he developed to empower individuals to separate from egoic thought patterns, embrace the present moment, and find fulfillment from within. Through his writing, guided meditations, and public speaking, Scott creates spaces where people can explore what it truly means to live with awareness, gratitude, and intention.

Scott's heartfelt dedication to improving lives extends beyond individual clients to entire communities, emphasizing the importance of balance and connection in today's fast-paced world. He believes that asking for help is a sign of strength and that every step toward wellness—no matter how small—is an act of courage. His work serves as a beacon of hope and resilience, encouraging readers to embrace their imperfections and rediscover the joy of simply being.

Part IV: The Paradigm Daily

The first seven days of the journal are included here. For the full 28-day journal, visit ImperfectionWellnes.com/Journal to download a free PDF copy.

The

Paradigm

Daily

A Journey of Self-discovery and Growth

Brought to you by Scott W. Possley &
Imperfection Wellness

The Paradigm Daily

The Paradigm Daily is a workbook and journal that you can have next to your desk or workspace. Keep it where it is easily accessible for you to write in when you have 5 to 10 minutes. The questions help reinforce the concepts of the paradigm until they become a new habit. The repetition of the questions help create new pathways in your brain to reinforce new patterns of thinking, hardwiring new behaviors.

At a minimum, I recommend doing some of the activities in the Daily Activity Guide each day, every morning when you wake up, and right before you go to bed. You are worth the investment, and I guarantee that you will feel better after a month of reinforcing these new behaviors.

The goal is to write in this journal for at least 28 days, though you can repeat it as often as you like. Download additional copies for free at ImperfectionWellness.com/Journal.

Daily Activity Guide

The goal of the daily activity guide exercises is to reinforce new associations with your thoughts and thinking patterns. We do not want to create a fake emotional experience. Instead, we want to reinforce present moment thinking, while addressing blocks, barriers or walls in our thought processes, which prevent us from feeling inner contentment and fulfillment.

Start each day with one, some or all of the exercises below, then go into the journal section. For the journal section, the first 7 days are included here to get your started.

Awareness Exercise
Start by bringing awareness to your thinking. Become aware that while you have thousands of thoughts each day, you are separate from your thoughts. Your thoughts may tell you that you are better than others or less than others. Your thoughts may tell you that there isn't enough to go around—be it food, housing, money, jobs, etc. Egoic thoughts give rise to never-ending commentary: judging, rating, and comparing you to everyone else around you. Instead of fighting this or believing this is you, just sit in awareness, knowing you have thoughts, and that you are separate from your thoughts. Be aware that the thoughts have no inherent meaning; instead they are half-truths, stories and fragments that the ego is feeding you. Bring your awareness to this without judgment or resistance, as humans have thousands of thoughts each day and you always will. Once you become aware of this, you are better able to utilize the other concepts in the paradigm.

Be The Observer Exercise
Sit for 30 seconds or more and observe your thoughts, saying to yourself, "I am separate from my thoughts and what they say about me and the world around me. I am going to watch you (the thoughts) and may even turn away from you since I am separate from you."

Come back to the reality of present moment, as you ground yourself and feel yourself in your chair. Watch the thoughts as a parade or clouds going by, or as a movie. Over time, observing the thoughts allows you to detach from identifying with what your thoughts say. You move toward, "I have thoughts and I am separate from them," as you move away from the fallacy of, "The thoughts are mine so they must be true."

Acceptance Exercise
Close your eyes for 30 seconds or more, and practice mindful breathing, focusing on your breath as you breathe in and out. As you do this, bring your attention to acceptance of everything, exactly as it is right now and as it was. This doesn't mean that everything is ok or that what happened was ok. Instead, you begin to realize and accept that what is or what was is unchangeable in the present moment. You sit with the discomfort of this and lean into acceptance. You let go of judgment—of good or bad, of being right or wrong—and feel the discomfort while breathing in and out.

While this feels uncomfortable at first, over time, it becomes empowering because you begin to realize you always have a choice and that your choices influence the future. As you do this, say to yourself, "I accept what is and what was in this present moment, knowing my actions today will influence my tomorrow. I may not like what is or what was, but I accept it as it is."

Note: When we are in judgment (and we don't judge judgment as it is how we have functioned for so many years), we are aligned with ego. Acceptance of what is and was without judgment is a challenge, but helps us come back to present moment living.

Reframing Exercise
See the reframing exercises on the next page and practice one or two daily as a daily affirmation.

Reframing Exercise

False Egoic Statement	Reframed as True Self
I'm not smart; I didn't go to college.	I am brilliant. I learn differently. Many successful people are not college graduates.
I am overweight, I am not good looking, I wish I had different hair, skin color, eye or nose shape, etc.	I compare myself only to me and I am aware that media and marketing want to tell me differently. I am beautiful exactly as I am!
I wish I were young again.	I find happiness in present moment and love the exact age I am. With my age comes knowledge and experience and I am exactly where I need to be.
I will be happy when "this" happens or when I have achieved "this" or have a new house, car, job promotion, etc.	I find my contentment from within, in the here and now, the present moment, knowing that I can make changes today that will influence tomorrow.
I wish I could do "x", but I am bad at everything. I just can't do anything right.	I can do anything I set my mind to. I set tangible goals and work towards them. It is an active process and if I work towards it, over time I can achieve it.

Write Your Own Reframing Statements

False Egoic Statement	Reframed as True Self

Mindfulness & Mindful Breathing Exercises

Bring mindful awareness to a simple task today, such as washing your hands, tying your shoes, or eating. As you do it, feel it fully, being completely aware of every step in the process. The easiest way to do this is to complete the task at half-speed. Engage in the process and appreciate each step, letting go of thought and judgment about what you are doing. Keep your awareness focused on this task for 30 seconds or more.

Alternatively, you can bring mindful breathing into any task or activity you are doing. As you complete the task, also bring your awareness to your breath, paying attention to your inhale and exhale. You will forget, and when you do, simply return your attention to your breath as you complete your task at hand, such as brushing your teeth, getting dressed, cooking or cleaning. Mindful breathing allows you to fully engage in present moment, creating space from your never-ending egoic thoughts. Over time, you can incorporate this practice throughout your day—while driving, sitting in a meeting, watching TV or engaging in any other activity.

Write your own daily activity below:

Mindful Breathing Techniques

1 Box Breathing

- This eyes open technique can be practiced anywhere, at any time
- While paying attention to your breath, inhale for a count of 4 seconds
- Then, hold your breath for a count of 4 seconds
- Next, exhale for a count of 4 seconds
- Then, hold for a count of 4 seconds
- Repeat this for 1-3 minutes several times a day

2 Mindful or Conscious Breathing

- This eyes open technique can be practiced while walking, cooking, cleaning, or doing other tasks. Associate it with a task to reinforce practicing it!
- While paying attention to the task at hand (such as brushing your teeth), gently bring your attention to your breath while you also complete the task
- Pay subtle attention to your breath as you inhale and exhale
- As you continue your task, continue to place your attention on your breath
- When you forget, simply come back to the technique as you complete the task
- Practice this throughout the day, associated with any task(s) you like

3 Eyes Closed Mindful Breathing

- Find a quiet place, sit comfortably, and close your eyes
- Take a slow deep breath, inhaling deeply through your nose, then exhale slowly through you mouth
- Now breathe naturally, allowing your breath to return to a natural rhythm
- Pay attention to each inhale and exhale, and when your mind naturally wanders, gently bring it back to your breath
- Do this for 3-5 minutes before and after work, and right before bed

4 Tips

- There is no right or wrong way to do mindful breathing. The fact you are doing it makes it right!
- You will have thoughts. This is normal. Once you realize you are having thoughts, simply come back to the breath.
- The goal is to start small. Try each one out and see which one you like best. Try one for a few minutes several times a day.
- Come back to Mindful Breathing daily. Within 30 days you will see a change in yourself!

The Checklist

Each day, choose one to three bullets and write them down as an affirmation of what you want to achieve. Read each one throughout the day as a reminder to reinforce a new pattern of thinking.

- I sit in acceptance of what is in this very present moment, letting go of regrets of yesterday and worries of tomorrow.

- I bring awareness to all situations and become the observer.

- I surrender to a power greater than and separate from me.

- I will forgive someone today, even if it is myself, for being human, knowing that humans are fallible and will make mistakes. I forgive so I don't have to carry the heavy emotional burden. This is freeing for me and doesn't mean what happened was ok!

- I will sit with the discomfort of a stressful or emotional situation and lean in, as I take a deep breath, and let go, knowing the discomfort will pass as the stored energy is released.

- I will do my best today. I may stumble and fall, but I will get back up. I will keep trying.

- What you (whoever "you" are) think of me is none of my business. What I think of me is none of my business. This is all ego passing judgments, ratings, and comparisons, so the information I get isn't helpful.

- I felt good scrolling through my social media today. If I don't, I will take a break and mute, delete or modify what I view so it is positive and leaves me feeling good. If needed, I will take a social media break.

- I know I always have a choice. I may not feel like I do, but I do. And choosing to do nothing is a perfectly acceptable choice. This can help take us out of any victim/martyr mentality we may have.

- I send love to myself and others, accepting us all as human—imperfections and all. There are many things I cannot change, so I begin by offering love and compassion to myself, letting go of judgment and comparison of myself and others.

- I drop the oars of the rowboat of life, letting go of control and the idea that I can control thousands of variables. I sit in present moment and mindfully breathe, knowing present moment is all we have in life.

Write your own below:

66

Life is not a struggle. The struggle is the inner conflict of what life is versus what we want it to be. Sit in acceptance and surrender, then set an intention and perform next right action.

~Scott W. Possley

Day 1   *Date:*   /   /

Daily Affirmation: Write an affirmation statement below. Repeat your affirmation 3-5 times each morning, night and throughout the day. Additionally, you can use the paradigm affirmation: I am Beautiful, I am Strong, I am Worth It, I am Enough!

Gratitude: List 3-5 things you are grateful for, and they can repeat as often as you like. Note: An easy gratitude exercise is to be grateful for each of your senses and what they bring you, e.g., I am grateful that I can taste my favorite meal, I am grateful that I can hear my favorite song, etc.

Day 1 Continued

Awareness: I become aware in this moment that I am separate from my thoughts. What are my thoughts saying right now? What will I do to separate from my thoughts? E.g., view them as a movie, as clouds going by, or as a parade going by. Write a positively worded reframing statement about becoming aware of being separate from your thoughts.

Acceptance of Present Moment: Am I fighting acceptance of everything that is, was, or will be? I will sit in the discomfort of acceptance for the next few minutes and feel the discomfort. If needed, I can perform some simple breathing exercises (see the Daily Activity Guide) as I become the observer and sit in acceptance. How did this feel?

Additional Reflection:

Day 2   *Date:*   /   /

Start your day with at least one of the activities from the
Daily Activity Guide Section

Daily Affirmation: Write an affirmation statement below. Repeat your affirmation 3-5 times each morning, night and throughout the day. Additionally, you can use the paradigm affirmation: I am Beautiful, I am Strong, I am Worth It, I am Enough!

Action Plan: What is my action plan for today if I get stuck associated with thoughts? For example, I will try meditation, an ice cold water plunge, walking around the block, 25 jumping jacks, other? See Chapter 13.

Present Moment Awareness: Am I living in present moment? Or am I 'story-telling' and creating a false narrative; judging, rating and comparing myself or others? Write a reframing statement, setting an intention for yourself, to come back to present moment. Performing mindful breathing as outlined in the "Daily Activity Guide" can also help.

Identifying Wins: What's one win from the last few days that I can celebrate? What challenge did I overcome or what have I achieved in the past few days? Include something you attempted or something you are working on that you are proud of. It can be something as simple as wiping the countertop or completing a school/work project. It is less about the outcome and more that you tried, creating a win!

Additional Reflection:

Start your day with at least one of the activities from the
Daily Activity Guide Section

Daily Affirmation: Write an affirmation statement below. Repeat your affirmation 3-5 times each morning, night and throughout the day. Additionally, you can use the paradigm affirmation: I am Beautiful, I am Strong, I am Worth It, I am Enough!

Gratitude: List 3-5 things you are grateful for, and they can repeat as often as you like. Note: An easy gratitude exercise is to be grateful for each of your senses and what they bring you, e.g., I am grateful that I can taste my favorite meal, I am grateful that I can hear my favorite song, etc.

Intention: Where I place my attention, or what I attend to, grows. Creating an intention, what I intend to do today in this moment, helps refocus my attention. What is my intention today? E.g., "I intend to align with my True Self by refraining from judging myself and others." Or, "I intend to heal and improve myself." Or, "I intend to start running and these are the steps I will take."

Judgments, Ratings & Comparisons: Do I need to let go of judgments, ratings (good vs. bad) & comparisons of self or others because I am attached to my ego and egoic thoughts? Am I judging, rating or comparing myself or others? Write a positive reframing statement.

Additional Reflection:

Day 4   *Date:*   /   /

Start your day with at least one of the activities from the
Daily Activity Guide Section

Daily Affirmation: Write an affirmation statement below. Repeat your affirmation 3-5 times each morning, night and throughout the day. Additionally, you can use the paradigm affirmation: I am Beautiful, I am Strong, I am Worth It, I am Enough!

Action Plan: What is my action plan for today if I get stuck associated with thoughts? For example, I will try meditation, an ice cold water plunge, walking around the block, 25 jumping jacks, other? See Chapter 13.

Day 4 Continued

Surrender: Is there something that I need to surrender? Is there an overwhelming feeling or situation that is more than what I can handle right now? Surrendering frees me from carrying the burden, knowing an answer or solution will easily come once I let go. Write a positive reframing statement for surrendering. See Chapter 9.

Lean In & Let Go: Is there a thought, feeling, emotion or experience that I am holding onto, fighting, avoiding, repressing or suppressing? What does letting go look like? How does it make me feel? How is my body responding? Write a positive reframing statement to support leaning in & letting go. See Chapter 10.

Day 4 Continued

Additional Reflection:

Day 5   *Date:*   /   /

Start your day with at least one of the activities from the
Daily Activity Guide Section

Daily Affirmation: Write an affirmation statement below.
Repeat your affirmation 3-5 times each morning, night and
throughout the day. Additionally, you can use the paradigm
affirmation: I am Beautiful, I am Strong, I am Worth It, I am
Enough!

Gratitude: List 3-5 things you are grateful for, and they can
repeat as often as you like. Note: An easy gratitude exercise
is to be grateful for each of your senses and what they bring
you, e.g., I am grateful that I can taste my favorite meal, I am
grateful that I can hear my favorite song, etc.

Forgiveness: Is there any person or situation that I am holding onto that is hurting me by carrying the emotional weight? Am I able to forgive (it's not about forgetting) so I can move on? I forgive for me, to set me free, knowing my forgiveness doesn't mean approving of what happened. Write a positive reframing statement. See Chapter 11.

Self-Compassion: Am I showing myself self-compassion? Am I in/was I in negative self-talk in the last day? What would I say/how would I treat my best friend or a loved one in a similar situation? Write a positively worded reframing statement. Note: If I can't show myself self-compassion, I become self-compassionate by being ok with my resistance. I choose not to judge myself or go into comparisons of what someone else might do.

Day 5 Continued

Additional Reflection:

Day 6   *Date:*   /   /

Start your day with at least one of the activities from the
Daily Activity Guide Section

Daily Affirmation: Write an affirmation statement below. Repeat your affirmation 3-5 times each morning, night and throughout the day. Additionally, you can use the paradigm affirmation: I am Beautiful, I am Strong, I am Worth It, I am Enough!

Action Plan: What is my action plan for today if I get stuck associated with thoughts? For example, I will try meditation, an ice cold water plunge, walking around the block, 25 jumping jacks, other? See Chapter 13.

Day 6 Continued

Hope: What am I looking forward to today or what goal do I want to work towards? What do I want to accomplish in the coming weeks, months or years? Note: We always want to stay in present moment, as our contentment & fulfillment is always from within, in the present moment, but this helps create hope and gives us something to work towards.

Abundance: Am I coming from an abundance mindset, knowing there is enough to go around, versus a mindset of scarcity, lack or not enough? Write a positively worded reframing statement with an abundance mindset, and incorporate some of your previous gratitude statements.

Additional Reflection:

As you look back at your week, there were likely many wins. There were also likely missed opportunities that we focus on, and we sometimes mis-label those as "failures." If you tried, then it's a success. If it was a missed opportunity, call it that instead of labeling it a failure.

Reflection Questions:

What accomplishments or milestones did I achieve this week that I am most proud of (and maybe include getting to this point in the journal)?

How am I celebrating and reinforcing these wins?

Day 7 Continued

What were some missed opportunities this week? Instead, can you celebrate them as wins, in that you tried?

What am I most grateful for in the last week?

Were there situations or experiences this week that challenged me to surrender or let go, let go of control over a situation or my environment? How did it feel to surrender or let go?

Resilience is quick recovery with agility to keep going after a setback. How was I resilient this week? How did it feel? If I wasn't resilient this week, what skills do I want to work on? Will I meditate more or utilize other breathing exercises like mindful breathing? Will I focus on surrender, forgiveness, or letting go?

Did you notice yourself getting associated with egoic thoughts or judging, rating and comparing? What next right actions (Chapter 13) were helpful in separating from these thoughts? What do you want to work on in the coming week when you becoming associated with your ego and its thoughts? Were you able to be the observer? Were you able to set an intention and perform next right action? If not, write an intention and action statement now:

Day 7 Continued

Additional Reflection:

Also by the author

Sam's life once brimmed with laughter and confidence—until high school hit. Suddenly, they're drowning in pressure and self-doubt, haunted by an inner voice whispering, "You'll never be good enough." Each day feels darker, and hope seems out of reach.

Then, in a single moment, everything shifts. Exhausted and teary-eyed, Sam accidentally knocks over Maggie in the hallway. Maggie sees Sam's pain and draws them into a circle of friends who offer understanding and a path forward. Sam learns to name their inner critic "Little Sam," while embracing simple daily actions instead of isolation.

Sam discovers Possley's Paradigm, learning the power of intention, the relief in speaking their truth, and the healing that comes from connection. Through bravery and raw honesty, they realize that self-doubt doesn't define them—and that hope was never truly lost. Raw and deeply real, this story explores the weight of teenage struggles and the light that emerges through compassion and courage while offering a roadmap to hope.

Beyond the Gray

A Journey of Overcoming and Belonging

by Scott W. Possley

Imperfection Wellness
Wellness for the PERFECTLY Imperfect!

The Imperfection Wellness Weekly Newsletter

Sign up for The Imperfection Wellness Newsletter, where you'll receive weekly insights, tips, and inspiration on everything wellness— from mindfulness and meditation to self-care and mental health.

As a bonus for signing up, you'll get these free wellness resources designed to help you live more mindfully every day:

- The Simple Guide to Wellness
- The Daily Gratitude Journal
- The Daily Meditation Tracker
- The Mindful Breathing Guide
- The Imperfection Wellness Prompt Journal

Stay connected, stay inspired, and take charge of your wellness journey! **Visit ImperfectionWellness.com/newsletter** and sign up today!

ImperfectionWellness.com

ImperfectionWellness.com is your go-to resource for holistic wellness and mindful living. Discover powerful meditation techniques, expert insights from Scott, and tune into The Imperfection Wellness Podcast for everything wellness or The Imperfection Wellness Guided Meditation Podcast for calming, transformative meditations. Start your journey today. Find your inner-peace and fulfillment from within and learn to live more authentically, one day at a time.

Download additional copies of
The Paradigm Daily
at ImperfectionWellness.com/Journal

Wellness for the
PERFECTLY Imperfect